Run, Mommy, Run

Run, Mommy, Run

Fighting Breast Cancer with a
Victor's Attitude

Gwyn Elizabeth Miller

Runspire, LLC
York, Pennsylvania

Runspire, LLC
Instagram: runspirellc

Book Production and Design by Cypress House
Dingbats © paci77/ iStockphoto

Publisher's Cataloguing in Publication
(Provided by Cassidy Cataloguing Services, Inc.)
Names: Miller, Gwyn Elizabeth, author.
Title: Run, Mommy, run : fighting breast cancer with a victor's attitude /
Gwyn Elizabeth Miller.
Description: First edition. | York, Pennsylvania : Runspire, LLC, [2025]
Identifiers: LCCN: 2025908243 | ISBN: 9798998735608 (paperback) |
9798998735622 (hardcover) | 9798998735615 (ebook)
Subjects: LCSH: Miller, Gwyn Elizabeth. | Breast--Cancer--Patients--
Biography. | Women runners--Biography. | Marathon running. |
Spirituality--Fiction. | Healing--Religious aspects--Christianity. |
Survival. | LCGFT: Autobiographies. | BISAC: BIOGRAPHY &
AUTOBIOGRAPHY / Memoirs. | BIOGRAPHY &
AUTOBIOGRAPHY / Survival. | BODY, MIND & SPIRIT /
Inspiration & Personal Growth.
Classification: LCC: RC280.B8 M55 2025 | DDC: 616.994490092--dc23

Printed in the USA

2 4 6 8 9 7 5 3 1

First edition

Dedication

For my Heavenly Father, whom I love with all my heart,
mind, soul, and strength.
Thank you for being my rock, helping me learn,
and not giving me more than you know I have
the strength to handle.

For Ken, my husband, who greatly loves me for
all my quirks and ambitions.
Through sickness and health is a vow you upheld well
with your loving strength and devotion, even when it
meant taking on both our roles. Thank you.

For my three beautiful, loving, and amazing children,
Trent, Aleya, and Derek,
you are and always will be my most precious gifts in life.

For my parents, Sandy and Gary, my in-laws, Larry
and Shirley, and my cousins, Jill and Ted, who traveled
from afar to help Ken and me navigate the weeks following
my double mastectomy. We appreciated your loving
assistance and support more than you know.

Table of Contents

Acknowledgments

Breast cancer has been my biggest adversary. Thank you to those who made the journey less daunting, cheered me on, and prayed for my recovery. While I might not have mentioned you by name here, I hope I made my appreciation known to you in my daily thoughts and words.

First, many thanks to my immediate family: Ken, my husband of twenty-eight years, and my three children, Trent, Aleya, and Derek. Thank you for making sacrifices, believing in me, taking care of me, and going with the flow when my illness disrupted all our lives. I loved how you stood strong and made me feel beautiful even when I lost parts of my appearance. You kept going even when I couldn't fulfill my role, and you didn't complain.

To my family, friends, and Ohio neighbors, whose limitless support, generosity, help with childcare, and prepared meals warmed my heart, you were my angels. I am so blessed to have you in my life. Your notes and prayers were the hugs I needed. May I never take you for granted.

To my Mt. Logan and Brunner Elementary School colleagues, who showed me that a work family is genuine and truly special, your outpouring of affection, donations, cards, gifts, phone calls, and meals made me feel so loved, sometimes to tears. Brunner, you proved that time doesn't matter when you're a family member. Once one, always one, no matter the distance.

All my teachers, from elementary school through college, have added something special to my life. Through their tutelage, I've gained much knowledge, insight, and direction, leading to my success. I would, however, like to acknowledge Mr. Richard Bowman, Dr. Thomas Getz, and Dr. Patricia Hinchey. Mr. Bowman, my most formidable high school teacher, taught me how to persevere and conquer challenges. When failing wasn't an option, I learned how rewarding studying eight hours or more for one test was and how achievement doesn't always come easy. Dr. Thomas Getz, my Penn State Writing for the Humanities professor in the early 1990s, restored my self-esteem as a writer. During freshman composition class at Penn State, I struggled to earn anything higher than a C, which led me to believe I had no writing talent. This changed when Dr. Getz inspired me, saw my talent, and kept copies of my work as great writing samples. Dr. Patricia Hinchey, my Penn State Educational Psychology professor, emphasized the importance of grammar, and made me the grammar czar for my master-class group projects. While I constantly sought perfection in my work and grades, she relayed how perfection is a slippery slope, and noted that while perfection is an honorable goal, it's not always attainable and can come at a cost to one's physical and mental health. These experiences and lessons learned have guided my path.

Without Ms. Julie McFarland, Mr. Frank Gaynor, and Ms. Cynthia Frank, I might not have attained my goal of publishing this book. To Julie and Frank, thank you for all your efforts in helping get my foot in the door at my first-choice publishing house. I appreciated all your updates as my book traveled through the process. While it wasn't chosen, I believe things happen for a reason. Thank you for suggesting Cypress House. Cynthia Frank has helped me reach my goal of publishing my work.

Last, I am most grateful to my healthcare team, who took extremely good care of me. These professionals from Columbus, Ohio's Mt. Carmel Women's Health Center and Hospital,

Adena Cancer Center, Surgical Oncology Associates, and Central Ohio Surgical Associates were a blessing. Thank you for giving me the best care and making me feel like your only patient. Thank you to surgical oncologist Dr. Brenda Sickle-Santanello, who continues to monitor my health during yearly checkups, Mrs. Suzanne Robertson, APRN-CNP, Dr. Greg Holland, plastic surgeon, Dr. Jeffrey Van Deusen, medical oncologist, Ms. Debra Bihl, chemotherapy education nurse, and the many nurses at the Adena Cancer Center (Chillicothe, Ohio) who took great care of me during four rounds of chemotherapy. Also, I thank Ms. Ellen Shinoskie, nurse navigator, who made the appointments leading up to my mastectomy seamless. Without her, I wouldn't have known about The Young Survival Coalition (YSC) website and would have had to take more sick days and car rides to Columbus. Finally, I thank Sue from CoreSource Insurance, who called weekly from diagnosis to the final chemo to check on my mental health and treated me like a friend, not an insured customer.

Chapter One

Nine Lives or Purpose?

The human mind may devise many plans,
but it is the purpose of the Lord that will be established

—Proverbs 19:21 (NRSV)

The first time I nearly died, I was six years old. My family had to deplane from our return flight leaving Los Angeles. Oblivious to why, I'm sure I was quite the angel in the airport during the late evening hours. As my mother recalls it, I wasn't. My father left her with three tired kids under age six while he went to check on flights. As a mom of three now, I'm surely biased when I say that my mom had a more challenging job. The many displaced and disgruntled passengers didn't herald the pilot—who refused when ordered to fly a plane with mechanical problems—as a hero; however, he was my hero when American Airlines Flight 191 crashed one week later. Had he flown the faulty plane, my whole family might have perished that night. To this day I'm grateful to that pilot. He was my first angel, an angel I never had the opportunity to thank.

My second brush with death happened in a car. After a monthlong stay with a host family in Salzburg, Austria, I returned home. Mom drove forty-five minutes to BWI airport to pick me up from my late-afternoon domestic flight from JFK following an international flight from Munich, Germany.

Suffering jet lag, I needed to sleep, but Mom wanted to chat. I felt awful about ignoring her, so I cracked open my eyes and participated in a little conversation. Then, as we rounded a curve on I-83 in Northern Maryland, I realized that a car in the slow lane in front of us wasn't moving. Seeing no driver, and with no time to spare before my Geo would slam into the gray Toyota, I yelled to my mother, "Switch lanes! Switch lanes! Move the damn car!"

Mom acted. She swerved into the fast lane and narrowly avoided the collision. Not needing to say, "Oh, my gosh" to acknowledge the situation's gravity, she did anyway. We were fortunate that no one was in the fast lane. As the adrenaline rush kicked my jet lag, our good fortune made me wonder: Would our near miss be someone else's direct hit? There were no flares, hazard lights, or cops to alert drivers to the disabled vehicle stranded in the slow lane. How could the Corolla's driver not have made other motorists aware of the potential hazard?

As if two near misses with death weren't enough, my third occurred on a gas-station sidewalk on a sunny Friday afternoon in downtown Chicago. Leaving the Rainforest Café, my cousin and I walked back to a parking garage. Suddenly, we heard the scream of police sirens. Before my cousin could ask why I was stepping toward her, a van plowed through the gas station at a 45-degree angle. Feeling a rush of air, I spun my head and saw maroon, only maroon, within inches of my face. If I hadn't moved toward my cousin, the van would have killed me—I'd have been a victim of a hit-and-run.

The van sped down an adjacent street, patrol cars in pursuit from all directions. It happened so fast it was surreal. The sirens faded, but we stood transfixed, our facial expressions questioning the incident. Once the shock dissipated and we could speak, we wondered what had caused me to move toward my cousin. Shaken, she mentioned not knowing my husband's cell number or where we had parked. I commented that no one in the gas station seemed bothered by my near-death experience, though given how quickly it had happened, they might have been unaware of how close to me the van had gotten.

As we began to walk, my cousin brought up guardian angels. She believed a guardian angel had pushed me away from harm and into her. Were angels able to dictate a person's movement? Wanting to believe, I questioned whether an angel could do so. Then again, weren't all things possible with God? Whatever made me walk into my cousin, I was thankful to be alive.

Occasionally, those brushes with death made me ponder: Why had they happened? Was there a purpose to them? How was I so fortunate as to be saved? Do we have an innate ability to take several falls and land uninjured, but does our fall count eventually expire? If not nine lives, like cats, then perhaps purpose? If this was so, why the need for near misses? Were they "get a clue" incidents meant to lead me toward the correct path?

Ultimately, we grace this Earth for a period unknown to us. While time is essential, we sometimes treat it as never-ending. When jeopardized or fleeting, however, time means everything.

Chapter Two

The Follow-Up

"And can any of you by worrying add a single hour to your span of life?"

—Matthew 6:27 (NRSV)

Having dropped my two-year-old son off at the sitter's, I drove up Route 124 toward Grove City, Ohio. I felt uneasy; my first mammogram was the catalyst. In 2009, Dr. Victor, my gynecologist in New Jersey, had suggested a mammogram for no reason other than to be proactive in my care. Since I was thirty-seven, I figured I had three more years before I needed this test. The initial mammogram was painful. I didn't realize it would feel like the machine was trying to tear my breasts from my body as it flattened each of them between two plastic plates.

Leaving the health center, I gave little thought to the mammogram until a few days later when I received a letter saying additional imaging studies were needed. Some areas required more mammogram films and sonogram studies for a complete evaluation. I'd have preferred to have seen the normal/negative result box checked, but the words "usually these findings turn out to be benign" eased my mind. I didn't let the letter or additional tests preoccupy me, but I became worried when told that a specialist needed to view my films and sonogram.

Amazing how the possibility of hearing that something might be wrong can turn one toward disbelief and despair. The night before my appointment with Dr. Beffler was long. Negative thoughts prevailed over my usually cheerful demeanor. Seated on the couch, my legs pulled toward my chest and a blanket to comfort me, I sobbed to my husband. I didn't want breast cancer. After finishing my master's degree, I wanted another baby. I didn't want people staring at me with pity. It was natural for people to be empathetic, but I wanted them to be able to look at me and feel comfortable. A cancer diagnosis would make me a victim. Though told not to worry until I knew, I struggled.

The next day, seated in Dr. Beffler's office, I faced a table full of magazines. These distractions didn't interest me. Conscious of my breathing, I waited. It was trying. What would the conversation be? Part of me wanted to know now, but another part wanted to leave and be oblivious. Naivety was blissful. A child's thinking, I know, but I wanted to live life as if everything were fine, whether it was or not. Unfortunately, I had no control over the news. Would I leave with knowledge of an illness changing my priorities, timeline, and outlook, or would I go home with a sense of relief?

A nurse called my name. I walk with her into the exam room where she left me with a gown. I removed my top and bra, put on the gown, then lifted myself onto the exam table. Dr. Beffler entered the room in a pleasant mood, which made me feel the news was positive. He placed two films onto the lighted view box and read them. Fortunately, it was good news. Due to my breast density, additional images were necessary, but based on what he saw, I was fine. He advised me to have a follow-up next year. I discussed wanting to have another baby. He said it would be okay to wait until the baby's birth for a follow-up mammogram.

Life flowed like a raging river rather than a babbling brook. Accepted into Penn State's World Campus Curriculum and Instruction: Children's Literature Program in spring 2009, I spent the next year and a half adapting to being a student, wife, mother of two, and teacher. With a grueling schedule, I found free time at a premium. Asked why I pushed to accomplish so much so quickly, I answered only that I had other goals to achieve. Actually, I wanted a third child. At thirty-seven, I wasn't getting any younger. May 2010 marked the end of my degree program with the revision and acceptance of my master's thesis. Following that, in June I found out I was pregnant. My husband learned of his job transfer to Ohio in July, and I graduated cum laude in August. Three weeks before Derek's birth, our house in New Jersey was on the market, and our first two showings occurred the day we brought Derek home from the hospital. Within two months, we'd moved to Southern Ohio.

In May 2012, a few months after I'd finished breastfeeding my third child, I had a gynecologist appointment and asked for a referral for a mammogram. My new gynecologist found no reason for me to have one. Finally, however, after I'd cited my age, nearly forty, and my previous promise to schedule a follow-up, he wrote the referral.

In June, I went for the mammogram. Hearing I'd finished breastfeeding in late February, the technician questioned the radiologist about whether she should proceed. To my annoyance, the radiologist suggested that a woman should wait six to seven months for a mammogram after having finished breastfeeding, which confirmed that I'd have to reschedule. The radiologist didn't want me to have a mammogram because my breast tissue might appear dense, which would make the film harder to read and interpret. She suggested I return in late September or early October to avoid inconclusive results.

Knowing I had driven an hour, the technician apologized and offered to send me a gas card. With permission from her supervisor, she wrote down my address and said to expect it in a week. Politely, I asked why this question hadn't been asked when I made the appointment. I'd answered many other questions. If it skewed results, whether you had breastfed in the past six months should have been a routine question.

I should have scheduled an appointment in the fall, but I delayed my return by accepting a fifth-grade teaching position. With no accumulated sick days, I needed to save the one and a quarter days I earned monthly to deal with my kids' illnesses, so I rescheduled the mammogram for the last day of winter break, January 3, 2013. After that, my older children would return to school, and I could leave my youngest with the sitter.

As I drove on a two-lane road and listened to '80s tunes, I allowed fearful thoughts to intrude. I tried to use the music as a distraction, but my mind swerved into dreary perspectives. What if I wasn't as lucky this time? Had I been proactive enough? When I raised my arms and circled the breast tissue from out to in, had I felt my breasts correctly? Wouldn't I have detected a problem? I convinced myself not to worry. I was the healthiest in my family. Indeed, training for marathons, eating right, and having no family history of breast cancer made me an unlikely victim.

As I continued to shove these thoughts out of my mind, I saw a state trooper pass me, headed in the opposite direction. The trooper made a U-turn three car lengths behind me. Crap! Was he after me? What was the speed limit? I didn't know. I looked down at my speedometer and saw that I was in the 50s, but had decelerated. Caught up in negative thoughts and predictions, I'd been paying less attention to my speed than to watching the road ahead. With two cars between us, the trooper followed behind. Was this a cat and mouse game? If he'd clocked me speeding, why didn't he turn his lights on, let the other cars move, and pull me over? Should I stop? I continued to drive and I looked for a speed-limit sign. There were none.

Suddenly the patrol car's lights began to flash. *Here we go,* I thought. I saw a farm ahead, and decided to pull into the front entrance, as the driveway had a wide delta-like opening, a safe place to stop. While I drove into the east gap, the trooper swung around into the west. His car faced mine. I turned off my motor, but kept the key in the ignition and turned it slightly so the radio played. As the trooper left his car, he looked all business; in fact he looked like the least pleasant person in the world, hardened and uncaring. Yes, this stop was leading to a ticket.

I lowered my window at his approach. He looked at me through his dark shades, and asked the typical question for a speeding violation: "Do you know how fast you were going?"

My answer, an honest no, meant little, as I knew he sought admission of guilt. To state why—my fear of breast cancer—as an excuse to avoid a ticket, was too personal. To him, my speed should have been my focus rather than whether today's mammogram would detect something abnormal. Instead, I rattled off a poor excuse about how I'd been listening to Don Henley's *The Boys of Summer* on my way to Grove City for a mammogram. Unfazed, he asked for my registration, insurance card, and license. I handed him all three, and he walked back to his patrol car.

Receiving a ticket should have aggravated me, but I calmly texted my husband. In reply, he texted that we would talk about it later. I texted back that there was nothing to discuss. I was at fault. Was this the start of bad things happening in threes? This was no day to start that chain. I hoped this was today's worst occurrence, and found solace in accepting a $115 speeding ticket. If anything, I considered it my donation to the Ohio State Troopers rather than a consequence of my actions. If good came from bad, then the ticket turned my focus back to being more conscious of the speed limit and my speedometer readings rather than breast cancer.

Fortunately, I was prompt. With no wait, I was led back to the same changing room as last time. I put on a robe, placed my folded clothing and purse into a cubby, and went to sit next to a plexiglass container. It held GRACE, a medium-sized, white stuffed polar bear whose name was an acronym for Guidance, Respect, Advocacy, Compassion, and Excellence. I felt as uncomfortable sitting next to her as I had in June. According to a card outside the box, breast cancer patients received GRACE. Next to the case, envelopes awaited donations. I'd considered helping subsidize the Mount Carmel Hospital Foundation Women's Health Fund initiative last time, but I couldn't shake the thought of my $25 donation going toward something for me—GRACE was an unsettling reminder of a mammogram's purpose.

The technician led me into the mammogram room. At the machine, I listened and acted on her instructions. First, she turned my body and maneuvered my breast correctly on the plastic plate. Then, from behind the screened-in area, she flipped a switch that activated the plates to squeeze my breast. There I waited for the discomfort I'd experienced in my previous mammogram. Fortunately, the pain wasn't as intense. Either the machines were better or my breasts were no longer as dense. Next, she took a series of different directional shots for each breast.

As I left the center, I wished for immediate knowledge. I hated waiting. I've always hated it. I managed, however, not to dwell on the outcome. On Monday morning, my cell phone rang. Usually, I let it go to voicemail while I drove, but I didn't receive many early morning calls. I thought it might pertain to one of the kids, so I answered. It wasn't about the kids; it was about me. The woman wanted to schedule an appointment for a diagnostic mammogram and ultrasound for the left breast. I tried to schedule it for the Friday before Martin Luther King Jr. Day when school wasn't in session. My attempt was fruitless. The office wasn't open on Fridays, so I chose the soonest available date, Wednesday, January 16.

When I'd hung up, I tried not to speculate. Until I heard the results, I wouldn't predict them. Nine days was a long stretch to be numb. They had my previous baseline mammogram. As I reflected on it, I remembered how calm I was between follow-up appointments; however, the night before the final analytic reading, I broke. I lamented over a possible breast cancer prognosis. What did fate hold for me this time? Would I have cancer? I wanted to be safe, but I had an ominous feeling that the results wouldn't be so easy to hear.

I walked into my classroom, placed my bag on my desk, grabbed my cell phone, and texted Ken about the follow-up appointment. He replied that he had a morning meeting, but could reschedule. I paused. While I wanted to believe this diagnostic mammogram would come back normal, I felt doubt. What if the news was bad? I texted how silly I would feel if he rescheduled the meeting and then I was okay. I did not, however, want to be alone an hour away from home if the news was distressing. As we texted back and forth with details, Ken left me with the words "Nothing could be more important." He was right.

Chapter Three

Say What?

Throw out the lifeline,
Throw out the lifeline,
Someone is sinking today.

—Edward Smith Ufford

I walked into the office, proceeded to the receptionist's desk, and gave my name as I removed my insurance card and license from my wallet. The woman's eyes darted back and forth between the computer screen and a few papers on her desk, and then she said I wasn't a scheduled appointment. I knew this was the correct date and time because I'd asked her to call my home phone and leave a message with the details. I'd played the recording last night, so I knew I was right. Why was I not on the list? Annoyed, I explained that I had taken a day off work and driven an hour.

She told me to wait, then entered another room to inquire about the mix-up. I shot a look toward Ken. He shrugged his shoulders, his hands open wide as if to ask, "What's going on?" I rolled my eyes, then returned my attention to the reception-ist's empty desk. When she returned, I asked her if I needed to reschedule. She said, "No, you need to be here," and continued to enter my information into the system. Her response made me suspicious. I looked at my paperwork for hints, but found it difficult to read upside down. Eventually, a nurse brought me back to a large waiting area with several changing rooms around its perimeter. She directed me to the first one, gave me directions, and walked off.

When I left the changing area, I sat alone. Breast-cancer pink, displayed through motifs and sayings on various articles such as T-shirts and posters, filled the room. Awareness messages enveloped me. It was disconcerting, almost haunting. I didn't want breast cancer to define me or be a part of my identity. It was hard to remain calm. As I tried to read Dr. Wayne Dyer's *The Power of Intention,* I heard staff members whispering in the hall. Was this the scene in a horror movie when the victim was oblivious to the imminent danger while the ominous music alerted the audience? Did the employees know? Were their whispers about me? Was I the naïve victim about to face a hellish situation? I strained my ears to listen to them, but could only decipher fragments. At one point, I thought I heard the word "young." I returned to the book and tried not to allow my mind to wander. I was going to be okay. Optimistic thoughts bred positive results—or so I hoped.

Brought to a mammography room, I followed the mammographer, who positioned me for proper imaging. I moved my head a right quarter turn. As the technician pushed me closer to the machine, she repositioned my left breast between the plastic plates. My hands gripped the metal bars. Modesty gone, I tried to make small talk to curb the awkwardness, but I could tell she wanted to stay professional rather than personal.

Afterward, I was led into another room and asked to lie on a table. There were two technicians in the room. One, who was helping train the other on the new ultrasound machine, asked me to hold my arm above my head to allow her to scan my left breast. She applied the warm gel, and then concentrated more on the right side of the breast than the left. I saw images of black-and-white lines and shapes on the screen, but was unaware of what she was trying to find. Slowly, she used her right hand to move the wand up and down and side to side along my breast while her left hand manipulated a ball-like mouse to move the cursor along the screen. Once she began to take measurements, I grew more hesitant and less hopeful that my breast was fine. I willed myself to remain calm, and pushed away negative thoughts.

The technician took several images, then moved the ultrasound wand toward my armpit. As she captured a few more pictures, I asked her if I could lower my arm soon, as it was growing tingly. Yes, she said, and apologized for my having had to hold it above my head for so long.

After taking measurements in all the requested areas, she departed, leaving the other technician to talk to me. Her words were disheartening. She discussed how one woman had wished for death after failing to detect her lumps. Then she spoke of how the patient should have caught it. Did she know? Had I, like that unnamed patient, failed to detect a lump? Always proactive regarding my body, I thought *No.*

I'd experienced similar discomforts three years earlier after my weekly kickboxing class. Ken suggested I had the flu, since I felt nauseated, lightheaded, and my body ached. I would have agreed if I hadn't had additional symptoms: My chest felt tight, which made it hard to breathe, and my arms tingled during the middle of the night. Rather than ignore the symptoms in hopes that they'd pass, I called the emergency room and spoke to a nurse who refused to offer a possible diagnosis. I understood. Liability precluded her giving me one. To avoid waking Ken and the kids, I decided to wait. I felt no better as morning dawned, so I had Ken take me to the ER once the kids were at school.

Once admitted, I explained my symptoms to a nurse and a doctor. After a chest x-ray, I awaited the results. When the doctor returned, he reviewed my vitals, said my chest x-ray was fine, diagnosed me with flu, claimed I'd had an anxiety attack, and said, "Your husband has a greater chance of heart problems than you have."

An anxiety attack? He knew nothing about me! Irritated and belittled by his comments, I was ready to leave. After the doctor exited, the nurse reentered and asked if I wanted Tylenol with codeine. Surprised, I told her it wouldn't be necessary as I had the flu. Equally surprised, she told me I had bruised chest-wall muscles, which caused the tightness I felt when breathing. Confused about why the doctor hadn't informed me, she said I'd made the right decision, and explained how a woman's signs of heart problems are vaguer than a man's. She reinforced her point by telling me that a healthy, active, thirty-six-year-old woman who'd been brought to their emergency room three weeks earlier, complaining of flu-like symptoms, had died of a heart attack. While a doctor called me anxiety-ridden, a nurse validated me. I'd known something was wrong then, but had I missed detecting something now? Had I neglected a warning sign?

The radiologist entered. He looked solemn. I mentioned that my husband was in the waiting room, and asked if someone could bring him so he could hear the test results. The technician left to get Ken, and my apprehension rose as the radiologist also departed. If everything had been fine, wouldn't he have said it was unnecessary to bring my husband in? Naivety kept me strong, but would reality break me? When the technician led Ken back, he and she took seats on opposite sides of the room while we awaited the radiologist.

When he reentered the room, he remained just inside the doorway and came right to the point. He said, "I'm concerned. I'm very concerned." I heard, "You have breast cancer."

This was the diagnosis, the blow, I didn't want. His words made me want to look behind me. Was he talking to me, the healthiest person in my family? How could this be? He continued his analysis of my screenings and the ultrasound measurements, then said that the diagnosis needed to be verified by a biopsy, but the shape of the cells was abnormal, like breast cancer.

In my white cotton gown, seated on the examining table, I was in disbelief. Health gone. An abnormality in my body called cancer. Why was this happening to me? My daughter, what had I passed on to my daughter? What about my students? Who would teach them now? What was I about to face? Looking dumbfounded yet calm, Ken sat in a chair to my left. Was he shaken? Did his insides churn as much as mine? What was he thinking?

The radiologist continued; I, however, remained at "You have breast cancer." Deafened by the words "breast cancer" that echoed in my mind, I failed to hear his evaluation of my films and ultrasound. My heart's manic beats relayed my stress level. Deflated, I felt a heavy sadness in my chest and a painful lump in my throat. Like a hand wringing a handkerchief, my mind spoke the words "Don't cry" while I tried hard to stay composed. The radiologist's face remained solemn and sympathetic as he discussed the two, possibly three, areas of concern.

Couldn't this be a fictional scene in a televised drama? I tried to summon the smart aleck tough guy who'd look over both shoulders before snickering, "Who you talking to? Me? Yeah, you ain't talking to me. You got it all wrong. I ain't your guy, so buzz off!" Instead, I felt pulled toward being the woman in a chick flick who sobbed and shrieked, "Me! Why me? What did I do wrong? Are you sure? You made a mistake, right? This sucks!"

It took all I had to control my feelings. I wanted to remain stoic, a pillar of strength, yet on the other hand, I wanted to lash out like a lion. Cancer, like a coward hidden inside me, had sent the radiologist, a courier, to forewarn me of its attack.

My attitude was boiling. I wanted to communicate a message of imminent defeat, and with piercing eyes stare cancer down. The fighter in me was ready to pummel it.

When the radiologist had finished, I slid off the examination table. Walking tall toward the door as Ken followed, I looked the radiologist directly in the eye and said, "Apparently, breast cancer doesn't know whose body it decided to attack, because I am a formidable opponent."

That powerful message meant my persevering and competitive attitude hadn't abandoned me. I've never surrendered to challenge. I loved movies where characters had to overcome adversity. When difficult situations arose during my adolescence, my dad would reiterate my favorite *Space Camp* movie line, "So competitive, aren't we?" He knew I'd choose to confront adversity with obstinacy. While shocked by the news, I meant what I'd said. Breast cancer was a rock in my path. Kick it or push it aside, I would remove cancer from my life's path. I would continue. Cancer would not.

While Ken went to the waiting room, I walked to the changing area with my belongings. I tried to look normal, though I wasn't. I didn't want other patients to sense my distress. Perhaps they too had a day coming that they would never forget. I closed the door and let my tears flow. In need of tissues, I found none, so I used my gown to wipe away the tears. I pulled myself together by concentrating on breathing. Next, I put the gown into the hamper and got dressed. Finally, I looked into the mirror. My eyes, red and glossy, signaled sadness and pain.

I left the changing room and turned down the hallway to the main lobby, wishing for no one other than Ken to be there. I wanted to talk, but an elderly gentleman three chairs to Ken's left denied my wish. I hid my face with my right hand and I leaned toward Ken to whisper my concerns.

When I heard the news, the first thing I thought about wasn't myself. I thought about Aleya, our daughter. What would this mean for her? What about the students I taught and was preparing for the OAAs? Who would continue to teach them? I didn't want what I'd worked so hard to accomplish to be ruined by my absence.

"Why me, Ken? I eat right. I run all the time. Why me?"

Ken remained quiet. He held my hand as we waited for a nurse to come and speak with us. I felt a sharp pang of grief, and needed a place to escape—the bathroom in front of where we sat. Again, no tissues! How could there be no tissues? I blotted my tears with a wad of toilet paper. I didn't want to cry, but found it hard to stop. I needed to purge myself of the sadness. Fighting a black shroud of torment, I wanted to be strong for the upcoming talk.

Shortly after I'd exited the bathroom and sat beside Ken, a nurse called us into a side room. There was a small table with four chairs. I sat in the one farthest from the door, and Ken sat across from me. I looked over my shoulder and saw a large display stand of pamphlets. One addressed how to tell your children about cancer. "Cancer" was such a scary word. How were we going to break this news to our children? How do you tell your thirteen-, eight-, and two-year-olds that you have cancer? How do you lessen their fears? I looked away and ignored my thoughts.

The nurse asked us if we had any questions. Questions? Still in shock, we had none, but we wanted answers. I had cancer, and I was clueless. When asked who my gynecologist was, I replied, "Dr. Villarreal."

The nurse called his office and asked for an oncology referral. She hung up the phone and grabbed a business card from among the many displayed on a shelf in the back of the room. She said, "Dr. Villarreal recommends Dr. Brenda Sickle-Santanello."

I took the pinkish-gray card with the breast cancer ribbon and looked at Ken who asked if she was the best; he emphasized that he wanted to know if there was a better choice. The nurse assured us that Dr. Sickle-Santanello was a highly regarded oncologist whose work was excellent.

Ken replied, "If she's varsity material, I'm fine with her."

The nurse said Dr. Sickle-Santanello's office would call us regarding our consultation date and time. Before we left, she handed me a sheet of paper with her name, the name of another nurse, and a phone number. We could call either of them if we had any questions. As we left the office, we remained silent.

With my head propped against the passenger-side window, I stared ahead as Ken headed the car home. I yearned for yesterday's innocence. I wanted solitude; I didn't want to talk. It wasn't a cure, but it would help me avoid the onset of more tears.

As we left the Columbus Beltway and drove south on Route 23, I remained stoic, watching the landscape pass by as my mind reviewed the day's discussion.

Processing: I am very concerned.

Processing: There are two or three areas of abnormal cell growth.

Processing: I have cancer.

Processing: To what extent?

Processing: Why me?

The tape replayed. There was no STOP button to press. I wanted it to stop. Finally, Ken interrupted it. He clasped his right-hand fingers tightly around my left. His touch, meant to be consoling and empathetic, induced my tears. When he asked if I wanted to talk, the dam broke and the flood came. I said no, and swept an arm across my eyes, but one swipe wasn't enough. I had to open the console and grab a tissue from a travel pack. I held the tissue over my eyes and let it all flow out. I'd held it long enough. A steady downpour saturated the first tissue; I reached for another.

Talk? No, I didn't want to talk! What I wanted was for Ken to pull off to the shoulder. I wanted him to stop the car. Hurt, I wanted to leave the car's confinement and run into the barren cornfield where I could displace my anger into the Earth's core. I wanted to scream, pull the wasting remnants of cornstalks from the dirt, throw whatever rocks I could find, and wield a stick upon a tree to relieve my pain. I remained silent, just looked at the barren field while I imagined these actions.

I wanted to be physically aggressive, but had no enemy to confront. Cancer was intangible. It laughed in my face and said, "Gotcha!" What had I done wrong? What preventative measures had I missed?

Fortunately, the drive home took an hour. Not wanting the kids to see me broken, I needed my pity party now so I could be strong later. I needed more facts and time to adjust before I told my children. Uncertain of my destination, I was in a holding pattern with no idea when I'd land or what I'd learn.

As the tears subsided, I began to talk. I discussed the need for privacy. I didn't want to tell our parents or our kids. If I decided to tell them now, what would I say? "I have breast cancer." Then what? Questions, questions with no answers, would follow. Responses of shock and despair would suffocate me like an avalanche. Snowed under by a lack of knowledge, I chose to hide my diagnosis. I had to address my reality before allowing others to know. It was imperative to learn more about my cancer first, so we agreed not to disclose the diagnosis. The oath of silence was my prerogative, and Ken supported my choice. Some might have seen it as a step toward denial. For me, the silence was necessary.

When we arrived home, I pushed aside reality. We held information that would change our family routine for an extended period, but my kids were none the wiser.

Chapter Four

Roulette

*For everything there is a season, and a time for every mat-
ter under heaven:
a time to weep, and a time to laugh; a time to mourn, and
a time to dance;...
a time to seek, and a time to lose; a time to keep, and a
time to throw away;...
a time to tear, and a time to sew; a time to keep silence,
and a time to speak.*

—Ecclesiastes 3:1,4,6,7 (NRSV)

Tired due to a lack of sleep, I was thankful for a professional development day followed by a four-day weekend courtesy of Dr. Martin Luther King, Jr. As I pulled into the middle-school parking lot, I received a phone call from Dr. Sickle-Santanello's office inquiring into my availability. For the next several months, Dr. Brenda, as I would come to call her, would factor in my life more than anyone. I requested the soonest opening. When I heard Tuesday, January 22, at 10 AM, I knew that taking the day after a long weekend and taking two sick days in less than a week would raise questions at my school; however, I wanted answers. I ended the call and texted Ken the appointment date and time.

I walked into the middle school and went directly to my assigned room for The Leader in Me training. Chillicothe City School District was Ohio's first Leader in Me district. The Leader in Me program used Stephen Covey's *Seven Habits* to develop leadership skills in students. Since Allen Elementary was the first in our district to implement it, Allen's teachers ran the training. The sessions focused on teaching each habit to our students through age-appropriate activities.

During the session for habit three, "Put First Things First," the presenters used a fishbowl in combination with big rocks and small pebbles. The pebbles represented the trivial things in life, while the big rocks stood for the significant ones. When the pebbles came first, there was little room for the larger rocks. The presenters showed, however, that if one planned for the most crucial parts of one's life to go first, then there was room for the smaller pebbles among the empty spaces. Then they handed out a sheet and asked us to reflect upon our big rocks versus small ones.

Self-reflection was the PAUSE button in a world on fast-forward. My life was always fast-paced, rushing to reach a destination or complete a task with little time between commitments and responsibilities. Multitasking was the norm, not the exception. The sands of time never ran slowly enough. Now picking up my pen, I had to analyze my rocks and pebbles. Habit three was a perspective exercise on priorities. Reluctantly, I wrote which stones took precedence in my fishbowl.

As I finished, I looked at my sheet. My big rocks were family time, being a wife, mother, and daughter, prayer, health, personal time, marathon training, my job, and time with friends. My little pebbles centered around cooking, cleaning, miscellaneous chores, and various motherly responsibilities such as taxiing my kids to sports, extracurricular activities, and helping with homework. All my answers felt important; however, had

I allowed my pebbles to squish out space for my big rock of health? Had I given myself enough hours of sleep each night? Remembering the many nights I'd fought off sleep to grade one more paper or stayed up into the early morning hours to tidy a house perfectly, I knew the answer: No. Had I eaten enough in the varied food groups for a healthy diet? Maybe. How many times had I sacrificed going to the gym because I was too busy after school and too tired after making dinner and putting the kids to bed? The numbers were too great. By not planning for essential rocks to be first, had I brought myself cancer? Had I too often placed others' needs and minor responsibilities before my own? I had. Retrospection sucks!

Asked to discuss our findings with our group, I wanted to keep my self-knowledge private. As I listened to others share how certain smaller pebbles took the space of a more crucial rock, I was ready to proceed to the next habit, and the presenter, as if reading my mind, granted my wish.

Throughout the day, I kept my pact and held my secret. When my past colleagues from Allen Elementary and the middle school asked how I was doing, I said, "Well." I lied. I smiled and laughed. I kept up a strong façade. No one knew, but I did, and it bothered me. I tried to ignore my new reality, but cancer came knocking every minute of every hour. It found cracks. It was resilient, and I was proving not to be. I believed privacy would give me strength, but perhaps not.

To conclude our professional development day, our super-intendent had staff assemble in the auditorium for one last presentation, a senior girl singing *Over the Rainbow*. I sat next to my fifth-grade colleague Cory. As I listened to the song about dreams, I thought about the goals I'd have to postpone, like running a spring marathon in hopes of qualifying for the Boston Marathon. As the girl sang in such melodic tones, my heart heaved, my eyes watered, and my thoughts drifted to cancer.

For a while, I suppressed my tears. Then, I leaned forward as if looking for something in my purse, swiped my shoulders across my eyes, and pulled myself together. After her performance, I left distraught.

Over the weekend, I distracted myself. My kids' sporting events, grocery shopping, mountains of dirty laundry, house-cleaning, and other ancillary activities kept my mind busy. Then, on a Sunday night, after the kids were asleep, I sat on the couch and read a book. After thirty minutes of rereading pages and not knowing what I'd read, I closed the book, walked to the kitchen desk, swapped my book for my laptop, and proceeded to the couch, my patience at an end.

I wanted answers, so I searched the internet. Though I knew it might be scary, I skimmed notable websites such as Susan G. Komen and the Mayo Clinic. Starting with the signs of breast cancer, I wondered what I had missed. I had done breast exams in the shower or lying in bed, but I wasn't consistent. I hadn't felt anything different; however, my breasts had undergone many changes due to pregnancy and breastfeeding. Their stretchmarks showed three rounds of childbirth. While I couldn't believe I had failed to detect it, I questioned why I would have. Never would I have thought I'd find cancer. My family bloodlines, except my mom's maternal side, had many ancestors who'd lived well into their eighties and nineties. In addition, due to my active, healthy lifestyle, I thought my body was resistant to such ailments.

As I looked over the well-defined stages, I recalled the radiologist's emphasis on three areas of concern, possible tumors; but I didn't know the size of these areas or whether they would be considered invasive or noninvasive. As for the lymph nodes, I knew the technician had taken ultrasound shots of my armpit, but the radiologist hadn't mentioned this area. Having read the descriptions, I assumed my cancer was either stage 1 or 2. The prognosis and statistics for survival of stage 2 were different from stage 1, but they were better than stages 3 or 4.

Seated in his recliner, Ken looked over at me. He saw me working on my laptop and asked what I was doing. I verified his suspicions, and he told me to stop. No! Like Pandora, I'd opened the box, only the box was a website. While Pandora closed her box in time to keep Elpis, the spirit of hope, I was losing hope.

Finally, Tuesday came, as did the typical morning routine: I woke the kids, prepared their breakfast, helped Aleya pack her lunch, and watched Trent and Aleya board the bus. Unlike a typical morning, Ken and I were headed to Columbus, not work. I changed Derek and packed the diaper bag, then double-checked whether my questions for Dr. Sickle-Santanello were in my purse. I remained calm as we left the driveway, and brought a book to keep me focused.

Ken asked if I was okay a few times during the drive. I knew he was concerned, but I was stronger than I'd been nine days ago. The shock had passed. Breast cancer was my temporary reality, and I needed to know how to rid my future of it.

We pulled into the parking lot fifteen minutes before my appointment, took Derek out of his car seat, and walked to the entrance. As we entered the building, I saw the doctor's office straight ahead. I opened the door and noticed a tank on the right side of the waiting area. Derek headed straight for it and spotted a turtle. He wanted to show me his find, so he motioned me to come. I walked over and stood next to him. He pointed to the swimming turtle, which swam toward me. It was enough to make me happy. Ken noticed how the little things in life made me happy. He was right—they always had.

Shortly after I'd registered, the nurse called my name. I followed her while Ken and Derek followed me. The nurse weighed me, took my blood pressure, asked me several questions, and left me with a gown and a medical checklist. After she shut the door, I changed, and then glanced at the medical questionnaire. I needed to identify any medical issues I had had or was currently having. In the past, I was able to check No repeatedly. Now, however, marred by my breast cancer diagnosis, my medical checklist was no longer an A+ indicator for perfect health. Robbed of my A+, was I an F now? How would insurance companies and doctors grade my health status? How far down the grading scale had cancer knocked me? When I reached remission, would my grade increase or remain at risk?

Dr. Brenda Sickle-Santanello entered the room, followed by Suzanne Robertson, her nurse practitioner. After introductions, a question and answer session ensued. Dr. Sickle-Santanello's questions, directed at finding the reason for my breast cancer, highlighted risk factors. How old was I when I had my first period? I was sixteen. When was my last menstrual cycle? Last month. Were my periods regular or irregular? They were regular. Did I smoke or drink? I didn't smoke, and drank only on occasions such as holidays or celebrations. When did I start birth control? I started at age twenty-four. What kind of birth control had I used? The pill, and most recently an implant. How long had I been on birth control? On and off for eleven years. How old was I when I had my first child? Twenty-seven years old. Did I breastfeed, and for how long? In total, I breastfed for nearly three years. Was there a family history of breast cancer? No. Ultimately, the doctor looked as shocked as I was when I first heard the diagnosis. I was an anomaly. She said that prognosis sometimes made no sense for certain patients, and cited a newly diagnosed patient who was a holistic eater.

Dr. Brenda placed my films on the lightbox and showed us the asymmetries and irregular areas of white that the radiologist had seen. She used a clockface to refer to the locations of the tumors in my left breast. One was at ten o'clock while the other was at eight o'clock. She asked me to lie back and began her examination to feel the tumors. She felt the ten o'clock tumor immediately but struggled to find the one at eight. Finally, she guided my hand to the ten o'clock tumor inside one of my stretch marks. It felt like a hard pea. She pointed to how the stretch mark appeared different, more puckered, than the others. After the examination, it was time to discuss treatment options and my list of questions.

My first question was what stage of breast cancer I had. Thinking I was stage 2 due to the number of tumors, I was happy when Dr. Sickle-Santanello told me stage 1. She explained that tumor size, whether the cancer was invasive or noninvasive, and whether it was in the lymph nodes determined the stage. While the ultrasound showed no indication of cancer in the lymph nodes, she suggested an MRI, which would provide higher-quality images and help check whether cancer had spread to the axillary lymph nodes in my armpits. If the MRI showed no cancer, a sentinel lymph node dissection during the mastectomy would provide the most conclusive data. Since we lived an hour away, and I wanted to avoid using another sick day, I asked if it was possible to have the MRI that day. She accommodated our needs and had her staff call to schedule an appointment.

Next, we discussed options. Through my Web search, I knew there were two surgical procedures. A lumpectomy removed the tumor and a small perimeter of normal tissue surrounding it, leaving the breast attached. In most cases, a single or double mastectomy removed the entire breast, including the nipple and areola. I wanted to be aggressive, and asked Dr. Sickle-Santanello for the best option. I was young and had young children to raise. She advised a double or bilateral mastectomy. When Ken heard her answer, he readjusted how he was sitting. We assumed a single mastectomy, not a double, would be necessary, so he questioned why. The doctor reasoned that my young age placed me at a higher risk for recurrence if I did a lumpectomy or single mastectomy. From an aesthetic angle, a double mastectomy would also allow for better symmetry during reconstructive surgery. Before the appointment, I wanted to keep my healthy breast, but based on her analysis and the percentage of recurrence in the other breast, I decided to have a double mastectomy. Ken was hesitant, but I was doing this once only. Saving a breast wasn't worth future worry and a possible repeat.

Afterward, I had questions about radiation, chemotherapy, and whether a hysterectomy would be necessary. Until the mastectomy was done, these answers were unknown. My tumors, the surrounding tissue, and the lymph nodes held the answers. A pathologist's report would indicate the size of the tumor masses, the cancer grade, whether my margins were clean, and my hormone receptor status. Radiation wouldn't be necessary if my lymph nodes and margins were clean. As for chemotherapy, it was too soon to discuss. My HER2 status would determine the potential need for a hysterectomy.

Three of my questions related to work. I knew I'd have to take a leave of absence, so I wanted to know when and for how long. I needed to notify my superintendent and principal so they'd have time to hire a long-term substitute. The doctor suggested performing the surgery in February or March. I wanted to make it through Ohio State testing, so I mentioned April. Too far away, this date placed me at further risk. My health took precedence, so I had to stop thinking like a teacher and more like a patient. In addition, I asked how much recovery time was required and about a return-to-work date. While four to six weeks was the average post-surgery recuperation time, my return date was undeterminable until the pathologist's report was available. If I needed chemotherapy, a return to school would be inadvisable, as my immune system, weakened from the drugs, would leave me susceptible to illnesses. In addition, chemotherapy could make one feel weak and tired. I decided to work until my surgery date.

My final question dealt with marathon goals. One of my resolutions was to run marathons in spring and fall of 2013 in hopes that I'd qualify for the Boston Marathon—3 hours and 45 minutes for my age group. I'd completed my second full marathon the previous fall with a personal best: 4 hours, 6 minutes, and 2 seconds. Having cut twenty-five minutes off my first marathon time, I felt Boston was within reach. When I asked about running marathons, she said, "Not this year." Though I heard her say no, my stubborn determination heard, *Anything is possible.* I thought, *Why not a third?* I would continue to run.

For the fine-needle aspiration, Ken and Derek left the room. The abnormal shapes indicated cancerous growth, which the biopsy would confirm or refute. The doctor gloved her hands, opened the sterilizing packets, and cleansed the area. On the counter, a biohazard bag contained two long needles. Always tough with needles, I had no fear. With each needle, I focused on the white ceiling tiles and felt only a tinge of pain. I felt an extracting sensation inside my breast for the ten o'clock tumor, but not with the eight o'clock. As Dr. Sickle-Santanello finished, a nurse knocked on the door to let her know she'd scheduled my MRI appointment, but I needed to leave immediately.

I made my next appointment for January 31 and received a small pink-and-black cloth bag. Once again, I faced the vexatious pink. There was no escaping the poster-child color. It was all around me in the office, down to the pink-covered breath mints. In the bag was a booklet of information I needed to read before our next meeting and a pink stress ball. I had no choice but to take it, but truly wanted to trash the gift bag because it felt like an anchor, a weight I wished not to carry. I placed the bag next to my feet in the car, then ignored it.

When we arrived at the center, Ken and Derek waited in the lobby while I followed the technician. As she discussed the MRI procedure, I filled out the forms, which asked questions similar to those I'd answered an hour earlier. Afterward, she took the paperwork and led me to a dressing room. Then I went into the MRI room. To help muffle the machine's pinging sound, the technician put earplugs in my ears and then helped me onto the MRI table. For optimal results, I needed to remain still. Lying face-down, I felt like I was on a spa table. Unfortunately, there was no masseuse. Once I was in the correct position, she put headphones that played music over my ears and put a clicker in my hand. To press the clicker would stop the MRI session, which meant we'd have to redo the session. There would be no clicking—I wanted results. Inside the imaging scanner, I heard a pinging that muted the music at times. It felt luxurious to rest, since I was sleep deprived, but I wished I could have had this time under different conditions.

After the MRI, we returned to Chillicothe, and arrived home before Trent and Aleya's bus did. I raced upstairs and hid the bag in my bedroom closet as if it were a Christmas present for the kids, but it wasn't a present, only a glaring reminder I wanted to ignore. I knew I wasn't strong enough to tackle what was inside the bag, so I pushed it aside.

Knowledge teetered me. Tension and fear eased up while confusion and aggravation pulled down. Pissed, I knew I would lose my breasts, but I didn't know what had caused my cancer. Cancer entered my life without permission, an unwelcome visitor, a criminal who trespassed on private property. Cancer's motive was unknown, so I began to investigate. My suspicions lay with the contraception implanted into my left arm six months earlier. Though told this was not the cause, I struggled to believe it. There was no evidence to prove my suspicions false. Nonetheless, I tried to piece together other possible scenarios.

Over the next week, I reviewed my preventative measures and genealogy records. At sixteen, I was the last of my girlfriends, and perhaps the entire sophomore class, to have my period. My pediatrician attributed it to my high level of physical activity. I started birth control in my mid-twenties, had my first child at twenty-seven, and breastfed all three children. A healthy eater, I was physically fit. As for genealogy, I reviewed my mother's maternal side, most affected by female cancers; no ancestors had ever had or died from breast cancer, but I wasn't sure about ovarian. Though I remembered my mom's recollection of her great-grandmother dying of a female cancer, I couldn't recall whether it was ovarian or cervical, so I reviewed my ancestry notes. Then I called my mother and cousin Jeannie to verify the information. Cervical cancer had caused my great-great-grandmother's death at age eighty-two and my great-aunt's at age fifty-four.

Next, I sought out statistics. According to Breast Cancer. org, about 1 in 8 American women, about 12%, would develop invasive breast cancer, one of the most common cancers and the second leading cause of death from cancer among American women. Though I wasn't in the less than 15% that had a first-degree relative diagnosed with breast cancer, was I in the 5–10% group linked to gene mutations, the most common being BRCA1 and BRCA2, inherited from my mother or father. While I knew that being a woman was the most significant risk factor, I was unaware that 85% of breast cancers occurred in women with no family history. For this 85%, aging and lifestyle caused genetic mutations. To add more fuel to my fire, I found that my having cancer nearly doubled my daughter's risk. Risk factors such as age, genetics, family, and menstrual history seemed irrelevant, as did the ones I could control, such as weight, exercise, unhealthy eating, pregnancy, breastfeeding, and alcohol or tobacco use.

Then I read about the many emerging risks: low levels of vitamin D, light exposure at night, and exposure to chemicals. While I appreciated the researchers' level of concern and the hours they spent searching for cancer causes, this was the worst Pandora's box. Had late nights when I fell asleep on the couch with the light on trying to complete graduate work or grade papers affected my health? As for chemical exposure, I was overwhelmed and thought about my late grandfather's statement when told he couldn't eat eggs and bacon for breakfast anymore due to his high blood pressure: "We are all going to die of something. I have been eating bacon and eggs for seventy-five years and am not quitting now."

Stubborn and unfeasible perhaps, but as I looked at the list of exposure to chemicals in cosmetics, food, lawn and garden products, plastics, sunscreen, water, and grilled, charred, barbequed, blackened, or smoked meats, I thought *Are you kidding me?* Indeed, we're all going to die of something. This list seemed to suggest that I live my life in fear. What kind of life is that?

Finally, I returned to the top suspect, birth control. I had used the pill for many years, and switched to an implant only after breastfeeding Derek. Before I'd chosen the implant, I read about the two types offered. Either insertion under the arm or into the vagina, but they were progesterone-only contraception. I thought progesterone was better than estrogen-based contraception, but it worked in tandem with estrogen. Dr. Sickle-Santanello disagreed with my suspicion; however, my cancer was only in the left breast, and the implant was in my left arm. No connection? I strongly disagreed.

Later, an evening news segment rekindled my anger. Researchers found that breastfeeding for longer than a year reduced a woman's chance of getting breast cancer more than in women who breastfed for a shorter time. Breastfeeding three kids, I nursed my first for eight weeks due to latching problems, my second for eighteen months, and my last for a year until mastitis occurred. The researchers' findings hadn't applied to me. Why not?

It seems I wasn't the only one questioning how I'd gotten cancer. Ken had his theories. A study he'd heard on the radio concluded that women who gave birth later were more prone to being diagnosed with breast cancer. In studies I'd read, a woman who had her first child late in life or had never borne a child was at greater risk. I had our firstborn at twenty-seven and our third at thirty-eight.

I hated being a random statistic, and found it difficult to stop searching, but spinning the roulette wheel of reasons was no help. I needed to walk away, but couldn't. I wanted an answer. Unfortunately, my case was a cold one. The factor, the definitive source of my cancer, was indeterminable. I felt like a kid who'd been given the word "because" as an answer. Why did I have breast cancer? Because a doctor and multiple imaging scans said I did.

I didn't want to be a cancer victim. It distorted my image and derailed my plans. Finding out I had cancer felt like I had dropped a mirror, cracked it, and predisposed myself to bad luck. Oh, how I wanted a new mirror, unbroken and unmarred. Cancer shattered my perfection. It riddled me with a sense of contempt and embarrassment. Perfection was prized, striven for, awed, and expected in America. Having to change my resolutions due to an illness was unacceptable. Was this God's way of telling me perfection wasn't a way of life? While He might have relayed the message, I failed to heed it. The news was like medicine, only the medicine wasn't going down. I was. What pulled me down were my whys, entrapments into solitary confinement. Why me? Why now? Why cancer? While the pleas reflected my confusion, the sentiment harbored disbelief. The questions were selfish. Why *not* me? What made me more special than anyone else? If cancer affected eight out of ten women, what made me so special as to be the two out of ten? Doesn't everyone have a chance to be the victim of an adverse event or the beneficiary of a positive one?

Chapter Five

Leaving Pity

*When you rise in the morning, give thanks for the light,
for your life, for your strength.*

—Tecumseh

W hen I returned to school the following day, a few of
my colleagues asked if everything was all right. They'd
noticed. My two absences in less than a week were a red flag.
I lied. I claimed Trent had had the flu last week, and Derek
followed with an ear infection. Guilty, I fabricated stories to
hide my truth. I didn't want to be deceitful, but silence was my
separation, the buffer between normality and reality, and private
versus public. Silence provided me time to accept, adjust, and
learn. Knowledge gave me power, enough to share with others. While I wasn't ready for all to know, one person needed
to know now.

Early Thursday morning, my phone rang. Seeing the 614 area
code of Columbus, Ohio, I took the call. Suzanne had my MRI
results. There were no concerns with my right breast, but the
left breast showed two masses, one at the ten o'clock position
and one at the eight. The largest measurement of the ten o'clock
mass was 1.5 cm.; the largest for the eight o'clock was 1.6 cm.

There were no abnormal lymph nodes on the right or left side, and both tumors were under 2 cm. in size; therefore, my cancer was stage 1. Areas of abnormal enhancement surrounded both masses, which suggested there was intraductal cancer, or ductal carcinoma in situ (DCIS), around each tumor. DCIS was non-invasive cancer considered stage 0. It starts when the abnormal cells grow and continue to grow inside the duct. Cancer becomes invasive when the abnormal cells break outside the milk ducts and invade nearby breast tissue. I was driving, so I asked her to call my cellphone again and leave a voicemail. I knew Ken would want to know the findings, but I feared I'd fumble some of the details Suzanne conveyed. She agreed to leave me a message and her cell number if I had further questions.

Having most of the information needed to answer questions, I emailed Jon Saxton, my superintendent, Thursday night, and requested a fifteen-minute meeting after school on Friday. Unfortunately, surgery was imminent, and long-term leave would be required. It felt awkward to tell the superintendent before my parents, but he needed ample time to find a substitute. After this disclosure, I would follow up with Elaine, my principal, because I assumed they would discuss potential substitutes.

Jon agreed to meet with me the following afternoon, but postponed and rescheduled our meeting for Monday afternoon. I understood. While my concerns were pressing, the school district faced a million-dollar fiscal crisis. As a result, the district focused on three cost-cutting options and a potential levy. Jon would have found time had I informed him of my meeting's intention; however, my needs didn't take precedence over crucial school-wide issues.

After the kids were in bed, I went into my bedroom and closed the door. For four days, I ignored the bag. Finally, I pulled the bag from its hiding place, brought it to my bed, took out the booklet, and started at page one. With each turn of the page,

I began to crumble. The diagramed drawings of a mastectomy patient with diagonal dash marks signifying the surgical cuts and the inset diagram showing the section of breast tissue, areola, and nipple removed during the procedure disturbed me the most. A mastectomy would alter my figure and leave scars as a reminder. Though hidden by clothes, it would not be hidden from my or my husband's eyes.

My tears intensified from a drop to a trickle to a cascade as I continued to read about mastectomy, sentinel node dissection, lymphedema, radiation, chemotherapy, and Tamoxifen. I hugged my pillows and used the sheets to wipe my tears. I knew it was selfish thinking, but I didn't want to do this. My concerns were about me, not my three young kids or my husband. My cowardice reemerged. I put the book back into the cloth bag, returned it to its hiding place, curled into the covers, buried my head into the pillows, and wept.

When Ken came to bed, I asked him to hold me. I told him I didn't want to face this obstacle. He praised my strength and perseverance while I felt weak and defeated. Why couldn't someone wake me? Vain, I didn't want to lose my chest. The permanency was disconcerting. I thought of 1 Corinthians 13:11 (NRSV): "When I was a child, I spoke like a child, I thought like a child, I reasoned like a child; when I became an adult, I put an end to childish ways." I thought how I had reverted to the selfish rationale of a child. Though I knew that to consider a single mastectomy rather than a double was risky, I was the child unwilling to relinquish the binky, blanket, or cherished stuffed animal. I had to cut those ties for my health, but my want controlled my reasoning.

The night rode like a rollercoaster: I'd wake and cry myself to sleep, then the morning would reverse my feelings. I awoke to the rising sun. Its rays embraced me as if to say everything would be all right. Throwing the covers over my head, I rolled

away from its rays. *What do* you *know?* I thought. Unable to
get back to sleep, I went to the bathroom. In the mirror, I saw
puffy eyes, signs of my inner war.

Helen Keller regarded self-pity as our worst enemy. It was.
In the past week and a half, I had lost rounds. My opponents,
cancer and self-pity, pummeled me. In my corner of the ring, my
conscience, my coach, yelled, "What are you doing out there?
Are you going to fight or go home? Quit or survive?"

Later that morning, my family and I attended church.
Though tired and feeling hollow, I dressed the part. As we
passed the greeters at St. Peter's Catholic Church, I took
a bulletin and smiled as they wished me a good morning.
I thought *If only it were.* It was easy to slide back into self-
pity, though I resolved not to. Pity, however, had a way of
ambushing my efforts.

I made my way to the pew and saw the cross, the dominant
image I saw every time I entered God's house, and a symbolic
reminder of Jesus' journey, persecution, and sacrifice through
death to save us from our sins. Funny, I was troubled with my
breast-cancer diagnosis, and Jesus carried humanity's burdens.
What would Jesus have thought of my self-pity? He would
have acknowledged my sorrow and then asked me to take up
my cross as he walked beside me.

Why? He understood. On the Mount of Olives, he knelt.
In the Garden of Gethsemane, he prayed, "Father, if you are
willing, remove this cup from me; yet, not my will but yours
be done." (Luke 22:42, NRSV).

Jesus felt anguish about his impending Crucifixion. Even
after an angel appeared and gave him strength, "he prayed more
earnestly, and his sweat became like great drops of blood falling down on the ground." (Luke 22:44, NRSV). Jesus suffered
knowing the plan. On the cross at "about three o'clock Jesus cried
with a loud voice, *Eli, Eli, lema sabachthani?*" that is, "My God, my

God, why have you forsaken me?"(Matthew 27:46, NRSV). In these biblical passages, Jesus was distraught. It was His Father's will, however, and Jesus accepted the mission.

Diagnosed with breast cancer, I felt forsaken. God had given me a cross to bear. A cross I didn't want, but it was God's will. Who says no to the Father? Jesus didn't. I wasn't about to either. Here to do His purpose, I would bear this cross rather than dive into a world of childlike behavior and protest that my cross seemed harder to bear than anyone else's. He knew me better than anyone, as evident in Matthew 10: 30–31(NRSV), which states, "And even the hairs of your head are all counted. So do not be afraid; you are of more value than many sparrows." In addition, later in that chapter, verse 38 (NRSV): "and whoever does not take up the cross and follow me is not worthy of me." I needed to heed the lesson Jesus modeled for us and know that my Father would care for me because Father knew best.

Seated in the tranquility of God's house, I accepted my breast cancer. Coming to church was like returning to my corner. My conscience had been right. I had to return to a winner's mindset to make myself victorious. Be the fighter, not the fallen.

Hadn't I put my gloves on with the statement "Cancer doesn't know whom it hit, because I am a formidable opponent"? I had, however, allowed that mindset to falter. My gloves had lain cold, waiting for me to reenter the ring, fists ready to jab, cross, hook, and uppercut. Cancer entered my house! I couldn't let it think it was okay to stay.

God knew I was a fighter and a survivor, but I had to acknowledge for myself what He knew all along. To fight and survive were the way of my cross, and I had to stop feeling sorry for myself.

After mass, I thought about what was to come. Better versed in the medical aspect, I was clueless about personal effects. Yes, I was going to lose my breasts. I knew I would need to remain in the house for a week after surgery and perform exercises to restore my arms' mobility and function. Then, for ten to fourteen days, I'd have to clean my drains and take baths instead of showers. Also, I couldn't lift, hold Derek, do housework, or run for four weeks. While I secretly rejoiced that I couldn't cook or clean, I knew it would make me feel useless and cause potential mayhem in our household.

It was clear I needed non-medical advice. How did I need to prepare? How much help would I require after surgery? What kind of discomfort or pain would I experience? I needed someone to answer these questions and more. Did I know anyone who'd gone through this? Who could guide me?

AnnMarie. I knew AnnMarie, a stage 2 breast-cancer survivor and previous New Jersey colleague who returned to teaching before I left for Ohio. Perhaps I could email her. I was hesitant. It had been a few years since we'd talked. Would she mind discussing cancer's aftereffects with me? Other than my deceased Aunt Rose, my cousin's mother-in-law, and my friend's mother, I knew few who'd been diagnosed with breast cancer. As a reference, she would be perfect. Like me, AnnMarie was a young mother when she was diagnosed. How would I start? After a few rewrites, I wrote:

Dear AnnMarie,

I know it's been awhile since I've been at Brunner Elementary. You're probably wondering why I'm writing to you. Unfortunately, it's not for a good reason. Last week, after a biopsy and MRI, I learned I have stage 1 cancer in my left breast. I'll be meeting with my oncologist again this Thursday to discuss treatment. While my right breast is unaffected, I plan to have a full mastectomy to avoid a recurrence. I haven't told anyone other than my husband. I'll inform my superintendent tomorrow and my principal the next day. I await information about the surgery date before I tell my parents and in-laws. As for my kids, I'll wait until the surgery is closer.

I'm writing to you because I want to know what it's like as a patient. I know you too were diagnosed with breast cancer at an early age, so I felt you'd be the best contact person for me. After reading the material the oncologist gave me, I still have questions. How are the first weeks of recovery? Will I be able to do anything? How incapacitated does the non-use of your surgical arms leave you? What do I need to do here at home to prepare?

My parents are seven hours away, and my in-laws eight. I know my parents would help, but my mom has AFib. I hope my in-laws will be able to come and help. Ken plans to stay home and help me for the first two weeks, but how long will I need help?

I'm sorry to burden you with this information, but I need a patient's perspective. Initially, it was hard to hear. I've had weak moments, but I'm a strong person. Mental toughness will come in handy. I won't bother you during this process. I need one conversation. Please call me at your convenience. Thanks so much. Please don't tell anyone at Brunner. Once I have more information, I'll send a note to fellow friends and staff members.

Sincerely,

Gwyn Miller

Later that evening, I checked my email. There was no response. I'd sent the message to AnneMarie's school account, and might have an answer by early morning or late afternoon. The following day, as soon as I awoke, I checked again. Sure enough, she'd responded.

Hi, Gwyn.

I just checked my email this morning. Of course I'll call you! Please don't worry; you're going to be fine. I had it in my right breast, and both breasts were removed (stage 2). I don't regret my mastectomy.

I'll call you today after school. Hang in there. It'll be fine. AnnMarie

As I left the house, I felt confident and ready to admit the breast cancer diagnosis, my secret, face to face with Jon. There would be no tears or signs of weakness. The morning was clear and bright, and my storms had passed. I awoke, a courageous warrior ready to fight my battle. Cancer was the enemy, but I smiled, knowing I would be the victor.

Chapter Six

Breaking Silence

Everything comes in time to him who knows how to wait.

—Leo Tolstoy

I t was apparent that Jon had questioned Elaine about my meeting request. Seeing me in the lunch line, she asked if everything was okay. I kept secretive, and told her I was. I hated lying, but felt Jon should know first, and the school lunch line was an ill-suited location to discuss my cancer.

Though slightly nervous, I felt at ease and strong as I drove to the administration building after school. I wanted to remain professional and straightforward with Jon. I had taken time to adjust to the news, knew more about the cancer, and had rehearsed this conversation. With each rehearsal, the lines changed. How do you tell your boss you have breast cancer? My husband advised me to be blunt. That approach could be rattling, but I decided he was right.

As I entered Jon's office, Jon's secretary told me Jon hadn't returned from a previous meeting, so I sat outside the office. Eventually, I saw him walk down the hall. He apologized for the delay, and I thanked him for his time. He didn't need an additional problem while he worked on passing an essential levy to keep our band program and avoid firing staff. He led me to his office and shut the door. I sat at a table in front of his desk, and he sat across from me.

"There's is no easy way to say this. I have breast cancer."

There it was, the look of utter disbelief. Jon folded his hands on the table. I informed him of my diagnosis, surgery, and estimated recovery time. I kept the discussion informative and calm, then smiled, reflecting my indomitable will.

Jon expressed shock and support, then asked whether I would resign. His tone reflected his wish that I not. Resign? My past job resignations were due to relocations; however, what options did I have as a first-year teacher in the district? Upon employment, I started with zero sick days and was therefore unable to join the sick bank. While I hoped to remain in the district, I had a one-year contract, and a RIF was possible. I said no, and I listened as Jon discussed my options for medical leave. Then he referred me to Missy in our personnel department. As the meeting ended, Jon emphasized his support by saying that I would be in his thoughts and prayers.

I'd felt calm and comfortable throughout that first discussion, and Jon had been attentive and empathetic. One conversation down, many more to go, but control over the timing, delivery, and message was mine.

Next I made my way to the personnel office. Missy was behind her desk. I told her Jon had referred me to her to discuss the options for taking leave due to cancer. She opened her bottom left desk drawer, pulled out a copy of our contract, and turned to the page on medical leave. Missy discussed the options: sick bank or medical leave under FMLA. Since I hadn't signed up for the sick bank, I could receive unpaid medical leave if I had a doctor's note that stated the needed recovery time. I could use my sick and personal days for paid leave, but I would need sick days for my kids and follow-up appointments in the fall. Missy handed me her business card and told me to write a letter to Jon to ask for medical leave due to my diagnosis and approximately how much time I'd need. In addition, I needed my oncologist to fax a note to Jon verifying the diagnosis and the required time for the surgery and recovery.

As I exited the administration building, I thought about AnnMarie and the multitude of questions I had for her. In response to her early morning email, I requested she call me after five o'clock if it wasn't inconvenient for her. I knew my after-school schedule was hectic: the 3:40 PM meeting with Jon; Aleya's 4:30 PM gymnastics team practice; and Derek's 5 PM pick-up. Our conversation would require privacy. AnnMarie replied I could call anytime, and gave me her cell and home number. I appreciated her time and knowledge because her advice was the additional insight I needed.

Initially, we played phone tag. As busy moms of active kids, our late afternoons into early evenings were hectic. As I prepared dinner while Derek watched TV and Trent did his homework, my cellphone rang. Fortunately, I had just put the chicken in the oven. To ensure that the kids wouldn't overhear our conversation, I ran upstairs to my room, locked the door, sat in my walk-in closet, and answered AnnMarie's call.

While I expressed my gratitude, she conveyed how glad she was that I reached out to her. First, we discussed her cancer story. Diagnosed with stage 2, AnnMarie had had cancer in her right breast and lymph nodes. She'd feared further progression, so she'd scheduled her surgery immediately, and chose a mastectomy with TRAM flap reconstruction. While my surgery required an overnight stay, hers had required a few days. Groggy from the medicine for the first week, she slept a lot, but she emphasized the importance of taking the pain medication. Since the ability to raise my arms toward my head would be weak, she suggested I buy a few button-down shirts.

Early on, daily arm exercises would be painful but would help return mobility. As for the drains, AnnMarie had needed help emptying them and had learned that safety pinning them to her surgical bra helped ease the weight. Finally, since she was HER 2+, an aggressive breast cancer that tests positive for a protein called human epidermal growth factor receptor 2, she'd had a hysterectomy. It was unknown whether I would need one, but I was willing to do whatever was necessary.

Eventually, AnnMarie attended her kids' events, such as her daughter's dance recital, to keep her home life unaffected. Still, she emphasized that help would be vital. It would be too much for Ken alone. He would need others. AnnMarie's mother had been a godsend, helping her with the household chores and childcare.

AnnMarie assured me that I would eventually forget the pain: "I don't regret my mastectomy. In the future, you won't either."

When I asked if I could call her again if I had additional questions, she said, "Of course." I thanked her and we said goodbye. The conversation left me feeling more prepared and at ease as a patient.

The next morning, I spoke to Elaine, who showed the same look of shock and disbelief as Jon had. Elaine listened as I reiterated the speech I'd given Jon plus what I'd learned from Missy. I discussed the cancer diagnosis, medical leave, estimated recovery time, and my uncertainty about additional treatments. While the initial timeline, end of February or beginning of March, was somewhat set, the ending was very gray. Since my kids, family, and friends were unaware of my diagnosis, I asked Elaine to let me take the lead as to sharing the information with staff and students. I was still gathering information, and wanted to shelter my kids and students, particularly the one who'd recently lost her mother to breast and ovarian cancer. I didn't want full disclosure. I didn't want to face sorrowful eyes, hear "So sorry" speeches, field questions about my diagnosis and treatment, or face pity. Elaine understood.

On a Thursday morning, I took my third sick day in slightly over two weeks, and Ken and I drove to Columbus to see Dr. Sickle-Santanello. While we waited for the doctor, Ken and I discussed the choice of mastectomy and the surgery date.

When Dr. Sickle-Santanello entered, she reviewed the findings of the biopsy and MRI. She believed that both tumors were cancerous, though the results came back conclusive for one and inconclusive for the other. Based on how the biopsy had felt, I agreed. I'd felt the penetration of the first tumor cell at ten o'clock, but didn't at eight. Fortunately, the MRI showed that my lymph nodes were cancer free. I remained hopeful that this would prove true during the sentinel lymph-node dissection.

Dr. Sickle-Santanello wanted me to do the buccal cell test, or swish test, to further assess why I had cancer. The DNA test analyzed my saliva sample for BRCA 1 and BRCA 2 genes. If I had those genes, then heredity might have caused my cancer. Even though none of my relatives had been diagnosed or died from breast or ovarian cancer, she wanted to rule out this factor. Before my diagnosis, I'd known of BRCA 1 and BRCA 2, the best-known genes linked to breast cancer, but had known little about how they increased the chances of developing breast and ovarian cancer. These two genes produced tumor-suppressor proteins that helped prevent cells from growing or dividing too rapidly and helped repair damaged DNA. DNA breaks, mended by BRCA 1 and other proteins, could occur due to natural and medical radiation, other environmental exposures, or when chromosomes exchanged genetic material in preparation for cell division. I thought these genes were most significant to developing breast and ovarian cancer, but I was mistaken. These altered genes accounted for only 5–10 percent of diagnosed breast cancers.

Next, we discussed a surgery date. With no family nearby, and hating to ask others for help, I knew it would be hard to determine a date. We were fortunate that Dr. Sickle-Santanello operated on Fridays, because Friday would be the most convenient day for others to watch our kids, so Ken and I requested the last Friday in February or the first Friday in March. The doctor chose to schedule my surgery for the last week in February, and had to check the availability of Mt. Carmel Hospital and Dr. Brian Holland, the breast reconstructive surgeon. I asked Dr. Sickle-Santanello if I could work until the day of my surgery, and she said it was my decision. Once the date was finalized, her staff would call to confirm my last day at work and write a medical-leave letter. She assured us that I'd be fine, and I believed her. Next, I needed preoperative testing and a consultation with Dr. Holland.

Before we left, a nurse handed me a 10mL trial-size bottle of Scope and a clean specimen cup. She instructed me to swish the mouthwash vigorously for a minute, then spit it into the cup. Afterward, I put the cap on the specimen cup, and the nurse sealed the lid with tape and wrote my name on the label. My saliva would be shipped to a laboratory and analyzed for the BRCA1 and BRCA 2 genes.

On our way home, Ken and I stopped at my favorite German restaurant, Schmidt's, in Columbus's German Village. Over lunch, we discussed sitter options, our parents, and disclosure. Since we'd need our parents for the second half of my recovery, we had to ask someone else to watch our kids. My Aunt Sue, who lived three hours away in Toledo, was our first choice. Ken and I decided to tell our kids and parents on Sunday. Then I would write a letter to family and friends, but I didn't plan to tell everyone. Ken wanted to read the letter before I sent it. I agreed. For some friends and neighbors, we would wait to share until after the surgery or longer. I wanted to be treated in the usual way for as long as possible. Ken guarded this request even more than I did.

The next morning, more colleagues asked if everything was okay. They'd detected that something wasn't right due to my recent string of absences, which was very unlike me. I appreciated their concern, but thanked them with lies. I told them that January had been a rough month for the kids. My only thought was to protect my family and myself. Three people knew, not including Ken and me. How long could I hide the truth? The more people who knew, the more likely the information would leak. I didn't want my kids to learn from someone else. Protection through procrastination was a weight I was willing to carry. I was like a momma bear, ready to do whatever it took to protect her cubs. Next to be informed would be Brenda and Cory, my grade-level colleagues, in case I needed their help.

Following the first period, we had a biweekly grade-level meeting while students were at specials. I shut the door and asked for Brenda and Cory's attention. Again, I was blunt. Their expressions mirrored Jon and Elaine's, shock and disbelief followed by concern. I told them about the diagnosis, my decision to have a mastectomy, and the as yet undetermined duration of medical leave. I asked for their silence. Brenda and Cory agreed, and offered their support.

With each meeting, I felt more at ease talking about my cancer, especially because the most difficult conversations were imminent. The past three conversations had been dress rehearsals. How I addressed my children about my diagnosis weighed heavily on me. The script kept changing. I sought a direct, honest, and upbeat conversation with Trent and Aleya, but wasn't sure how to prepare Derek, who was nearly two. As for our parents, Ken and I had decided to speak to them. I knew my dad would be stoically calm, but wasn't sure how my mom, a worrywart, would handle it, so we decided to have the conversation on Sunday.

Sunday came. We decided to wait. We didn't want the news to affect Trent's basketball-tournament performance. Also, we should have thought about Super Bowl Sunday. With my parents at Dad's cousin's house, I didn't want to diminish the party mood or have the talk center on me. In addition, Ken didn't want me to handle the kids' emotions while he was away on business. Our excuses bespoke avoidance, but another week wouldn't matter.

I relished the delay. Telling my parents meant telling my kids. Once my parents knew, the news would spread to my siblings. I didn't want my older son and daughter to learn of my diagnosis from my nieces and nephews through social media. Cancer held negative connotations. While everyone's experience with it was different and outcomes varied, the disease bred fear. I preferred to tell the kids as close to the surgery as possible because I didn't want them to be worried, think the worst, or lie awake wondering whether their mother would live or die.

On Monday, Susan called with my swish-test results. BRCA 1 and BRCA 2 weren't present in my genetics; thus heredity hadn't predisposed me to cancer. Relieved yet baffled, I yearned for a reason, but searching for the source of my cancer, something I might never discover, was a waste of time. The reason wasn't worth the strife. The journey toward an answer stopped then and there.

Chapter Seven

A Runner's High

*There are no impossible obstacles;
there are just stronger and weaker wills,
that's all!*

—Jules Verne

No one in my family ran. Gymnastics introduced me to running at age eight. Later, I joined my parochial elementary school's cross-country team, took a hiatus during junior high due to a move, and ran varsity my freshman through senior years. After high school, I occasionally ran until the birth of my second child. Then my competitive nature returned, and I began to participate in several 5K and 10K road races. Following Derek's birth, I ran Kill the Hill, a ten-mile race in support of a local landmark, the Adena mansion, and the Columbus Marathon, a fall race that supported the Nationwide Children's Hospital. My husband thought running a ten-miler in June was too much after I'd had a baby in February. As for a marathon, Ken reminded me that the farthest I'd run was ten miles, and suggested I start with a half marathon, but telling me, the stubborn, determined one, that I can't do something only fueled my fire.

In high school, my answer would have been no to a marathon. Had I ever thought I'd be a breast cancer patient? No! Life isn't a controlled variable. One can make plans and set goals, but sometimes life interferes. I began January with a New Year's resolution to compete in two marathons and make Boston's qualifying time, but sixteen days later, my resolution met breast cancer. Loosening my hold on the reins, I knew a spring marathon was impossible, but my inner Superwoman told me to run and shoot for the fall.

Fortunately, my marathon training had preceded the diagnosis. God knew what He was doing when He set the goal of running a marathon in my mind. Marathon training requires mental and physical strength, and mental strength is the ultimate key to survival when life hits below the belt. Your performance falls flat if your thoughts aren't in synch with your ability. As for mental strength, I thought I'd already achieved my belt weight. Going for a new record, ready to take it on or not, I had a weighty challenge that I hadn't sought but needed to tackle.

"Grueling" described marathon training. The time commitment was intense. My eighteen-week program consisted of running four days a week, one cross-training day, and two days' rest. Mileage ranged from three to ten miles on the weekday runs and eight to twenty miles for the weekend run. That long run, which took one to three hours, was taxing. Runs that exceeded fifteen miles left my quads and thighs extremely sore. Add a baby jogger and the weight of a Derek while I ran up Chillicothe's steep inclines, and I had an upper body workout. I ignored the pain of tired legs, and sacrificed sleeping in on Saturday. My want was deep.

The 2011 Nationwide Children's Hospital Columbus Marathon, my first, was beyond what I'd imagined. The morning was cold, but I kept warm at a heated bus stop until I needed to enter Corral C. I felt like a cow in a cattle chute, but the excitement

was high. Speakers spoke, and a singer sang the national anthem.
A huge American flag hung atop a giant cherry picker. When
the countdown reached zero, a cannon shot, fireworks, and AC/
DC's *Thunderstruck* started the race. Two hundred meters or
less behind the starting line, my run began as a walk, which led
into a jog. As runners neared the starting line, sweatshirts and
garbage bags were tossed aside. I crossed the line and I started
my Garmin as Springsteen's *Born to Run* began.

Personal space was tight, with nearly 10,000 people entered
in the half and almost 5,000 in the full marathon. The first few
miles were bob and weave as I tried to keep my pace and move
forward. Distractions were all around. Cheering, high fives, and
supporters holding signs lined the streets. The themed patient
champion mile stations were moving. Each themed mile, chosen
by Nationwide Children's Hospital patients who ranged in age
from birth to eighteen, began with a mile marker that showed
a patient's picture, name, age, and illness. Then, the patient, his
family, and friends rallied, passing runners from a tented area
near the mile-marker sign.

Mile 13, a slow incline, was mentally challenging. Here a left
arrow on a lighted road-construction sign signaled the turnoff
for the half marathoners, while marathoners proceeded straight.
As the half marathoners neared their finish, the crowd's cheers
intensified. The course and the cheering section became less
dense for the rest of the teen miles. At mile 17, I began to tire
as I crossed the bridge and headed for the loop around the
Ohio State stadium, but I kept pushing, focused on the finish.

At the Expo, speakers discussed how runners hit a wall during
the last third of the race. When I reached mile 20, I hit invigora-
tion. I held back tears of joy. With 6.2 miles left, a weary body, a
slowing pace, and achy knees, I felt my drive and smile intensify.
Then, I saw a half-mile sign on a tree. At first, I was excited to
see the sign, only to eventually loathe the person who'd put it

there. Amazing how something so short can become forever long. With every turn, I wanted an end.

When I saw the word FINISH in white letters on a lime-green background, I sprinted. It was a beautiful sight. Arches of orange, blue, and white balloons celebrated my achievement as spectators behind metal barriers shouted, rang cowbells, and waved signs. Using the downhill, I sprinted toward the digital clock and the black rubber timing mat. As I crossed, I heard nothing. It was a Whitney moment, an actual *One Moment in Time* when time stopped. As I walked, my legs, heavy and strained, ached as I moved toward the volunteer who handed me a Mylar blanket. Another gave me my finisher's medal, while a third gave me bottled water. Finally, I made my way to greet my family in the Athlete's Village area.

The 2011 Columbus Marathon, meant to be a one-time accomplishment, inspired me to race again. Shaving twenty-six minutes off my record the following year made me contemplate Boston. Couldn't I shave another twenty to qualify?

Even though a spring marathon was no longer possible, I continued to run. Running was an energizer that helped me combat sadness. When I ran, I was a fighter. Pounding the pavement, I saw my running course as the ring, my feet as my fists, and the road as my punching bag. My cheering section, the lyrics of my fight songs: *Not Afraid* by Eminem, *The Fighter* by Gym Class Heroes, and *I Won't Back Down* by Tom Petty, roared through the earbuds of my iPod. Daily running kept me focused. Another illness was brewing, however, and it wouldn't knock me out, but it would make me feel like I was hanging on the ropes.

Chapter Eight

Traversing the Valleys

*The marvelous richness of human experience would lose
something of rewarding joy if there were no limitations to
overcome. The hilltop hour would not be half so wonderful
if there were no dark valleys to traverse.*

—Helen Keller

To help decrease the number of sick days I used for trips to
Columbus before surgery, the oncologist scheduled both
my preoperative testing and plastic-surgeon consult on February
7. I appreciated the thoughtfulness. On arrival at the hospital,
I parked, rode the elevator to the third floor, registered at the
desk, sat in the waiting area, and began to read a recent copy
of *Educational Leadership*. Only an older gentleman and his
wife sat across from me until a nurse brought two women into
the waiting area. They sat to my right, and while I tried not to
listen to their conversation, I overheard. They were preparing
for gastric bypass surgery.

How was I the one with breast cancer? Hadn't I taken care
of my body? Why should a woman who ate well and exercised
often fall victim to such disease while other women who lacked
caring for their bodies avoided such a pitfall? Evil? Yes! Rude?

Absolutely! Unchristianlike thoughts? Indeed! My aggravation didn't care about political correctness or "Love thy neighbor as thyself." Their negligence of their health fueled my anger. Having to face the unlikely consequences to my lifestyle sucked. As fast as the evil thoughts came, I left them, returned to my own business, and focused on reading.

Eventually, I was led to a room where I sat on the examination table. As she took my blood pressure, the nurse apologized for the delay. Rather than stay on schedule, she had listened to a distraught prostate-cancer patient. I assumed she meant the older gentleman I'd seen earlier. She grabbed the office chair, wheeled it over to the computer, and asked the same litany of questions my oncologist had. As she entered the information into the computer, she noticed that my surgery date was March 1 at 8 AM.

Afterward, Ellen, the nurse I'd met on the day of my initial diagnosis, came and walked me to radiology for a chest x-ray. I was fortunate that she did, as it was a circuitous route. When we'd walked into the waiting room and sat down, Ellen pulled a binder labeled Young Survival Coalition (YSC) from her bag. Then she asked for my test results and asked the same questions I'd answered earlier, but this time, Ellen wrote my answers in the binder. She emphasized the importance of keeping records for future reference, and handed me the binder as she finished. I flipped through the binder, and saw it contained additional literature and the YSC's web address—website tailored to the needs of young women, ages forty and under, diagnosed with breast cancer.

Next, Ellen handed me a pamphlet for Images for Women, a cancer boutique adjacent to Mt. Carmel Hospital East that offered a wide assortment of surgical bras, breast prostheses, and swimwear. She suggested I be fitted for and buy two surgical bras. Following my mastectomy, I'd need to wear the surgical bra—a compression bra made of elastic fabric with a hook-and-eye closure in the front—day and night during the recovery process until the incision scars, tissue, and skin had healed.

Called back for bloodwork, I left Ellen only to sit in another chair. Though the previous patient had left, phone calls took precedence. I watched the minutes on my phone move swiftly toward my consultation appointment with Dr. Holland. I thought an hour between appointments was sufficient since he was in a medical building attached to the hospital, but I was wrong. Worried, I dialed Dr. Holland's office and spoke to one of his receptionists.

Unbeknownst to me, I had a personal assistant for the day, Ellen, who Amanda said had already called to inform them I'd be late. After the bloodwork, Ellen showed me the walkway to Medical Building #3, but her favors didn't stop there. She scheduled a surgical bra fitting for me at Images for Women, so I had adequate time to see Dr. Holland and make it home before Trent and Aleya's bus arrived. As we parted, Ellen said she'd call me later in the week to see how I was doing. I thanked her in appreciation for making the process smooth and stress-free. With Ellen, I knew there was no need to worry—I was in great hands.

I greeted the receptionist, signed in, and gave her my insurance card. Earlier in the week, she emailed me the new patient forms, which I'd completed and emailed back to her. The nurse called my name, brought me into an examination room, and gave me a folder that contained three pamphlets and an informational background sheet about Dr. Brian Holland. After glancing over Dr. Holland's bio, I skimmed the pamphlets. Each outlined the types of reconstructive surgery and showed the various types of implants. Through AnnMarie and Dr. Sickle-Santanello, I was aware of a few choices. I read about the TRAM flap, latissimus dorsi flap, and implants. When I saw the flap diagrams and read the captions, I preferred the tissue expander followed by silicone or saline-filled implants. Though the reconstruction process would be lengthier and require additional surgery, I didn't want more scars, and flap reconstruction would leave scars across my stomach or back. In addition, flap- reconstruction recovery time, according to the pamphlet, wasn't as easy. As for silicone implants, I feared health risks. Silicone made me think of cancer. According to the brochure, clinical studies demonstrated no link between silicone-gel implants and cancer. Still, I was leery.

With a smile, Dr. Holland entered. Shaking my hand as he introduced himself, he sat on a stool and moved toward me. His calm, caring, and professional demeanor put me at ease. Holland looked the part. Immediately, I asked which reconstructive surgery he would suggest based on my body type and active lifestyle. He recommended reconstruction with expanders followed by implants since I was lean and fit. I agreed. Worried about health risks associated with silicone breast implants, I asked him about my concerns. He said that breast implants were much safer than they were several years ago.

He used a diagram in the pamphlet to explain the tissue-expansion reconstruction process. First, he would place an expander, the same width as the original breast, beneath my chest wall muscle. Then, to stretch the skin gradually, the expanders would be filled through the filling ports. Finally, he showed me where an acellular dermis allograft, made from donated human tissue from cadavers, would be placed. Like a sling, the allograft provided extra support for the implant. Once the expansion process was complete, implants would replace the expanders. Unlike bra-cup sizes, implants were cubic centimeters or ccs. He opened a drawer and showed me several different-sized implants and allowed me to hold them. Since chemotherapy damaged implants, the final surgery to replace the expanders was contingent on my pathology report. Recovery time was two to three weeks, and I could run once I recovered. As for sensation, it differed in all patients. Some had more sensation return in the breast area than others.

With all my questions answered, I left the hospital and headed to Images for Women. I entered and saw a vast dark waiting room, but no one was there or behind the desk. *Too quiet.* I wondered if I'd come during lunch break. Then I saw a woman looking for someone and said I had a bra-fitting appointment. She asked me to sit in a chair while she went in to inform the sales associate. She returned, and said the associate was with a customer and would be with me shortly. After an older woman with two other ladies left, a saleswoman welcomed me, and I thanked her for fitting me into her schedule.

She brought me back to a changing room and asked me to remove my shirt and bra so she could measure under my bust and the fullest part of my chest. Given that my breasts would be gone, I wondered why this was necessary. After measuring, she handed me two white surgical bras, sizes 38 and 40, to try. I removed one from the package. Its thick material had straps an inch and a half wide with a frontal hook-and-eye closure. I knew it was temporary, meant to serve a purpose, but its purpose, far from pleasure, made me feel old. As the saleswoman explained that the bra should feel snug and the band comfortable, I held it up like a specimen.

I grimaced. Eww! My sexy factor plummeted to below freezing. As if losing my breasts weren't enough, I had to wear an old-lady bra. What would I do with my dainty, lacy, sexy bras and lingerie, and the newer bras I'd bought before my diagnosis? They were useless! I could no longer wear underwire bras. In addition, since implants came in ccs, my fake breasts wouldn't be a cup size. How would I fit myself into a bra? Would I be condemned to sports-like bras or the ones that came in small, medium, and large? Best cancel my Victoria's

Secret credit card; my modeling days were over. My sexy just died—give it a funeral!

I began to connect the several hooks and eyes. When I looked in the trifold mirror, I saw it cover my chest. I felt like I was wearing a life vest, but this one pulled on me like an anvil, a weight of ugly. I was drowning in unattractiveness. Since the bra fit, I took it off and returned it to the packaging. I appreciated my current bra, which hugged my God-given voluptuous breasts as I dressed. Over the next few weeks, I would vainly admire my bras and breasts since they would soon be useless and gone, respectively. The road map of my body was about to lose a pair of curves that my husband and I deeply prized.

While the saleswoman put my two surgical bras in a bag, I wondered if I had enough time to shop for button-down shirts. I drove to the nearest discount retail chain with less than an hour to spare. I found a shirt rack, slid the hangers from right to left, and grabbed the first five button-downs I liked. I tried one size too small, and noted whether the material was comfortable in the arms and slightly stretched in the front. I wanted the deep purple, burnt orange, and blue-and-white-striped shirts, so I returned the other two to the rack and proceeded to checkout.

I made it home to pick Derek up from daycare before Trent and Aleya stepped off the bus. After my motherly duties— taxiing Aleya to gymnastics and coming home to prepare dinner before I'd return to the YMCA to pick her up from practice—I put the kids to bed. Then I emailed Jon and Elaine.

Dear Jon and Elaine,
   Fortunately, an incredible team of doctors and nurses accommodated my schedule needs, so I could complete my preoperative testing, meet with the plastic surgeon, and purchase post-surgical wear. It was a full day.

The nurse recording my vitals saw my surgery scheduled for Friday, March 1, at 8 AM. My plastic surgeon's staff was unaware of the date, so I await confirmation from Dr. Sickle-Santanello. Friday is her scheduled day at the hospital, so I should hear back by Monday. If March 1 is the assigned date, my last day will be Thursday, February 28.

Jon, I shall have Dr. Sickle-Santanello's staff fax you to verify my medical leave time for the mastectomy. The pathology report will determine whether further treatment is needed. Chemotherapy and radiation, if required, will prolong my final reconstruction. In addition, I won't be using all my sick days or personal leave because I'll need these days when I return. I know this isn't definitive, but I wanted to inform you of what I've learned.

Sincerely,

Gwyn

During the week, Ken and Derek caught colds. I washed my hands religiously, kept my distance, and went to bed early, but I too came down with a cold. Ken and Derek were better within days, but I battled the symptoms for over a week. By Valentine's Day, I had lost my voice. My throat hurt so bad that I thought I had strep throat. Fortunately, we had a class party in the afternoon, because teaching with no voice proved impossible.

I needed to see a doctor. With Ken traveling, I called my babysitter and two older children to tell them I would be late. As I drove to Urgent Care, I prayed there would be few to no people. I saw very few cars in the parking lot, walked into an empty lobby, and thought *God loves me*. I told the doctor that I was scheduled for breast-cancer surgery in two weeks. He examined me, found that I had sinusitis and bronchitis, and he prescribed a five-day zip pack of amoxicillin, a twelve-hour cough syrup, and an expectorant.

Though I took my medicine and went to bed early, I felt no better on Sunday. Any exertion led to uncontrollable coughing fits that ended at times in dry heaves. It helped to rest and drink water, but with just one more day's medication, I thought *Why am I not better?*

I went to church anyway. There were Sundays when I struggled to apply the homily to my life because the message sometimes seemed to speak to others. This morning's homily, however, spoke to me. It was as if God knew I needed to hear His message. After he'd read Matthew's gospel, Father Bill Hahn delivered a sermon focused on the number 40. He discussed how, in biblical stories, that number stood for a period of struggle or strife, a time of testing. For example, Noah built an ark to survive the forty days and forty nights of rain. Moses was on the mountain with God for forty days and nights. The Israelites wandered the desert for forty years. Jesus fasted in the desert for forty days. The forty-something time of trial and testing ended with a period of renewal or revival. Ironically, I was forty. Was God suggesting this was my struggle? I believed He was.

I didn't know why God had chosen me for such a struggle, whether it was intended for me or for me to model for my children. Though I thought God had given me challenging moments in the past, He seemed to be telling me I could handle a little more. Could I?

Chapter Nine

Full Disclosure

It's not what happens to you, but how you react to it that matters.

—Epictetus

As the weeks progressed toward my surgery, rumors had begun to circulate, so Brenda advised me to tell the rest of the school staff. I appreciated her concern but even though people would talk, I exercised the right to hold my information until I was ready to make it public. Besides, Ken and I had yet to tell our parents and the kids.

We didn't want negative feelings to hover over Derek's birthday celebration on Saturday, so we decided to wait until Sunday. We tried to orchestrate the perfect moment, and kept pushing the talk to a later date. There would never be an ideal time to disclose the news, because worrisome news has no perfect moment. Saying it was as hard as hearing it.

As planned, we told the kids on Sunday evening. I sported a smile as I sat on the couch; Aleya and Trent faced me, and Ken sat off to the side in his recliner. With the mention of the frequent doctor's appointments, Trent had assumed our news was about a new baby. If only.

To assuage their worry, I first explained that when a woman turned forty, she needed a mammogram, so I had scheduled one. A machine had taken pictures of the inside of my breasts. The images of my left breast images concerned the radiologist. Further tests found two tumors smaller than 2cm. I mentioned the tumors were cancerous but had been caught early, so this was positive.

Next, I discussed the operation. I explained that the best option to stop cancer was to remove both breasts even though one was healthy. After the procedure, I'd need help because I wouldn't be able to lift or do much else until my wounds healed. Whether I needed further treatments, such as radiation or chemotherapy, would depend on what my doctor found.

Then I emphasized that they could ask us any questions about my cancer, but only us. Since cancer experiences and outcomes differed from person to person, I didn't want information based on someone else's knowledge and type of cancer to cause them needless worry.

I presented the information clearly and calmly, and ended with a few pep-rally statements. I praised my excellent doctors, told the kids I believed all would be well, asked for their trust, and asked if they had questions. Aleya had more than Trent. Both wanted to know how long I'd be in the hospital and what would happen while I was there. They asked whether they could still visit their cousins this summer, and wanted to know who would watch them while Ken and I were away. Inquisitive and bold, Aleya posed an aesthetic question about my chest. Ken looked uneasy and went into protective mode; he felt the question was inappropriate. I wanted the kids to know I was open, honest, and okay. I felt it was right for Aleya to understand the truth, so I answered that I would be flat until a plastic surgeon rebuilt my chest. There were some questions I couldn't answer, but I promised them I would answer them when I had more information.

The talk had gone well, better than I'd anticipated. With surgery two weeks away, the children had little time to dwell on it. Since Trent was older, had seen my Uncle Terry die of cancer, and had a classmate who was undergoing chemotherapy, I imagined that he'd struggle with the news more than Aleya, who had a sweet naivety and strong faith in me. They seemed unaffected, but I wondered *Are they hiding their fears? Are they worried, or have I convinced them that all would end well?*

Ken had already called his parents, but I hadn't called mine. This responsibility weighed hard on me. I wanted to avoid it. Ultimately, I didn't want my mother to cry. Parents worry. I'd never known how real this was until I became one. Even though my youngest son would say, "No worry, Mommy, no worry," I still stood guard, and watched and spotted his every move on the playground equipment. As a mom, I wanted to protect my children from pain and sickness, but mothers don't possess this power. We can nurture, but we can't ensure perfect health or guarantee safety.

While I was a mother, I was a child too, a child who was about to tell her parents she had stage-1 breast cancer. I hated knowing I would cause worry. I wanted to shield them, but protector wasn't my role. Secrecy wasn't the answer, because there was no hiding cancer. My illness would become apparent. My phone call would deliver the message "Don't worry, I'll be fine," but I knew my words would fall flat. I was their daughter. The one they conceived, raised, cared for, and continued to love.

Hearing the ringtone, I thought, *How do I start?* I hoped they weren't home, but knew they were. Mom answered. I wanted Dad to hear me, so I asked her to switch to speaker. As I spoke, they were silent. Ken's parents had taken it hard; they couldn't understand why this had happened. I assumed my parents' reaction mirrored theirs. I envisioned my mother holding back tears next to Dad, who'd be composed and strong but inwardly worried.

My mother insisted on coming. I was hesitant due to her AFib, but I accepted, knowing Ken would need assistance. Next, Mom asked whether we needed them to watch the kids during my surgery. I explained that we would rather have them come out the third or fourth week of my recovery, since Ken was handling the first two. As for the surgery, I explained that my cousin Jill and her husband, Ted, would help us with the kids during my surgery and hospital stay. I said that Aunt Sue, Jill, and Ted were our best choices because they lived nearer to us. While Aunt Sue, who was retired, would have done it, she had outpatient surgery the same day. Fortunately, Jill and Ted agreed to come up on a Thursday night to watch the kids; they planned to leave on Sunday unless we needed them longer. I ended the conversation and asked Mom and Dad to relay the news to my sister and brother.

After I'd disclosed the news to my parents, in-laws, and kids, I wanted to inform additional family members and friends. It would have been arduous and emotionally draining to call, so a letter, though less personal, was the best option. It needed to be concise, and share my medical details and emotional state. I drafted a note and shared the rough copy with Ken. After a few revisions, I sent the following email.

Dear Family and Friends,

On January 3, I had my forty-year mammogram. On January 16, I learned I had stage-1 breast cancer in my left breast. The following week a biopsy and MRI confirmed the tumors. After a meeting with the oncologist, I decided to have a double mastectomy and reconstructive surgery. I chose the double based on my age and removing the possibility of a recurrence in the other breast. The surgery is on March 1 in Columbus, Ohio.

This came out of nowhere. No one in my family has a history of this type of cancer. I hadn't detected it before the mammogram either; however, 80% of breast cancer cases are not hereditary. I did the BRCA 1 and BRCA 2 genetic testing, and the results were negative for a gene mutation for breast and ovarian cancer. The why remains a mystery, and I've decided to let it stay one. While the first day I learned of the news was hard, I'm fine now. Breast cancer did not realize whom it was attacking, because I am a formidable opponent.

As for further treatment, I won't know until after the surgery. First, the pathologist will have to dissect and analyze the tumors. I might need radiation or chemotherapy based on the tumor and sentinel-node findings. The MRI didn't detect any cancer in the lymph nodes, so hopefully, the node testing during surgery will prove the same.

I am very private and like to deal with problems on my own and within my family, but many of you might be hurt if I didn't share this information. I'm not one for having people fuss over me, as it's usually my job to take care of others. All I ask is for your prayers and that you not worry. Please don't feel you have to call. I'm physically sick, but I'm fine mentally. I'm not scared or distressed. I have excellent doctors and am blessed to be under their care. As I learn more, I'll keep you updated.

I am a strong-willed and positive person. I believe my marathon training will benefit me during this time. It's an intensive physical and mental training period, so I'm not concerned with the fatigue or side effects cancer might bring. I'll get through it. God has always looked after me, and I don't expect it to be different now. He knows what He is doing. As for the patient side, I have a friend and past colleague diagnosed with stage-2 breast cancer in her late thirties when her kids were five and seven. She's been instrumental in helping me understand what I'll face as a patient, so I now have an outreach person.

Sincerely,

Gwyn

I clicked the SEND button, and contemplated how the recipients would react. I foresaw surprise followed by sadness. I hoped the responses wouldn't relapse me into self-pity. Sometimes words can grasp the soul in unexpected or unwanted ways. Having sent the email near midnight, I shut down the computer; I knew there would be no immediate response. My letter unleashed a burden. With my mind at peace, I slept well.

Responses came, and a few questioned a double mastectomy. I understood their sentiments because I'd been there. Love and concern overshadowed logic. Others saw strength in my words and were unsurprised by my steadfast and inspirational attitude. Many offered prayers and support. Some messages brought tears; others fueled my spirit. My favorite was from Heather, my cousin Jimmy's wife. She wrote:

My dearest Gwyn:

First of all, I applaud how strong you are and your tenacity to hit this evil disease. You inspire me, and I want you to know I want to be a part of your journey. You bring such truth and uplifting inspiration to a time when most people would crawl under a rock. Whatever you, Ken, or the kids need, please tell me. Let us know our weekend to come down and help. We are walking arm and arm with you in this.

I remember when my mom learned about her breast cancer at age forty-two, where I am now. Now I find from you how to live past this disease, move forward, and live for every moment. You have embraced how shit hits the fan and have blown the mother up with your fight.

Gwyn, we love you dearly and have many prayers and well wishes flooding your way. You are my brave inspiration, and I will wait for news when you have more or want to talk.

Love much,
Heather

In addition, I sent a shorter version of the letter to my principal, and asked her to forward it to staff members. While I considered sharing the news face-to-face at a staff meeting, I wanted to avoid burdening colleagues with the additional time away from their families and responsibilities. I asked staff members to refrain from telling the students. I wanted to maintain a positive classroom environment, and planned to remain silent until the day before my surgery. Unfortunately, I had to approach the music teacher, who'd told a few students, and reminded her not to discuss my medical issues with any of the students. I didn't want them to worry.

Throughout the workweek, a few colleagues came to my classroom. I wasn't shocked when Kathy Murray, a breast-cancer survivor, came to offer support. Their sentiments and concern were endearing, but I made it known that I was okay. I knew I would be fine. Breast cancer was a bump in my road, but I planned to move beyond it. While I answered their questions, I smiled, cracked jokes, and appeared confident. I was. It might have sounded crass to joke about turning in my old chest for a new one, but sometimes one must laugh at the absurdity of circumstances. Joseph Campbell said, "As you proceed through life, following your own path, birds will shit on you. Don't bother to brush it off. Getting a comedic view of your situation gives you spiritual distance. Having a sense of humor saves you."

Indeed, laughter was my medicine. My gaiety was a slap in cancer's face. It wanted to strip me of my happiness, but I wouldn't let it. Negative thoughts and attitudes afforded me no luxuries, so why stray into that barren land? Through the Bible, God teaches that we reap what we sow, so I decided to bring happiness and positivity to this struggle. I wanted to reap these in my life.

While I believed in God, I failed to believe in the unexplainable, like signs, due to my skepticism. Beliefs can change, however. Mine did. On a Saturday morning, on my way to the laundry room, I saw a candle Ken had lit earlier on the stove. I knew it had been burning for several hours, so I blew it out. I saw the wick go black, and I went to the laundry room. After I'd folded the laundry from the dryer, I left to put the clothes in our rooms. When I came back downstairs, I saw a lit candle! Who had lighted it? Ken was upstairs, Aleya was watching TV, Derek was asleep, and Trent volunteered at the SPCA. Stunned, I stepped back; I knew I'd blown the candle out and had seen it go black.

While I wanted to question and dismiss it, I couldn't. I had witnessed a sign from God. In John 8:12 (NRSV), Jesus said, "I am the light of the world. Whoever follows me will never walk in darkness but will have the light of life." He wanted me to know He was there. I was going to be okay. How did I know? Jesus' light told me so.

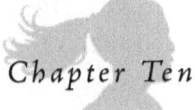

Chapter Ten

Receiving Grace

Health is the greatest gift,
contentment the greatest wealth,
faithfulness the best relationship.
   —Buddha

As a child, I celebrated every Christmas Eve at my grand-parents' house in Toledo. After the Christmas Eve church service, I was anxious to arrive so I could play with my cousins. Once we'd eaten and the kitchen table had been cleared, we gathered around my grandparents' Christmas tree, covered with multicolored lights and red velvet ornaments. We kids, young-est to oldest, opened our presents first, followed by the adults. My grandparents, always last, made it a point to express how spoiled they felt and how unnecessary the gifts were. To them, their health and happiness were the most important gifts. Their insight was wise. No one could buy health and happiness. Those who possessed such riches should treasure them.

My health was a trainwreck. Usually, I might see a doctor once a year due to bronchitis. Otherwise, I was a healthy person. Now I'd come full circle. With cancer, I was seeing more doctors than ever. My coughing fits continued, even with medication, and any exertion led to uncontrollable coughing. The removal of contraception caused night sweats, which made me take showers in the middle of the night. During the week, I suffered chills due to a 102° fever. Too weak to reach the bathroom, I woke Ken when I felt I would get sick. I felt awful. I wanted my health back. I was a boxer hanging on the ropes, not officially down but hearing the count.

Unable to get an appointment with my doctor, I went to Urgent Care again. I saw the same doctor, told him the medicine wasn't working, and said I needed to recover quickly so as not to postpone my mastectomy. Instead, I wished to have the cancer removed before it worsened. This time, the doctor prescribed a more potent penicillin and multi-symptom allergy medication. I hoped these new meds would help.

As my health improved, the time to prepare grew short. I went to bed early, but had hectic teaching days. I prepared lessons for substitute teachers, and stocked up on toiletries and nonperishables. I wanted a thoroughly clean house, so I tried to do spring cleaning before I became unable to help. Ken told me to take it easy, but I focused on everything being in order. I wanted him to have as little to do as possible. I knew that what he was about to face would be overwhelming. The coughing fits, however, though decreasing, made me slow down. To stop them, I had to rest. It was God's way of making me take a break; He knew I wouldn't unless I had to.

On the day before surgery, I was in overload mode; I tried to finish my sub plans and information binder, cleaned my classroom, and readied myself to talk to my students at the end of the day. Twenty minutes before dismissal, I had my colleagues, Cory and Brenda, bring their homerooms to my classroom. I smiled as we conversed and I answered their questions. I didn't want to instill fear or panic, so I was vague but truthful. I told the students I'd have surgery and wasn't sure whether I would return to the classroom before the year ended. My return depended on the surgery and what doctors found and prescribed as my treatment.

Then, I left the classroom. I wanted to relax but had much to do. While my substitute binder fell short of my perfectionist criteria, I'd done what I could. I needed to trust that Pam, a retired Chillicothe elementary teacher, would do the rest. I had to pick up Derek.

Jesse, Derek's sitter, was waiting outside with the boys. It was hard to pull Derek away from JJ, his best friend, until I started to converse with Jesse. Amazing how quickly children seek your attention when it's no longer on them! Jesse offered to help whenever I needed her over the next four weeks. I thanked her and put Derek in his car seat.

When I reached the house, I dropped Derek off for the older two to watch until Ken came home. Then I loaded bags of laundry, detergent, and fabric softener into my car. Earlier in the week, our washer had broken. Once again, I thought of Mother Teresa's words about God not giving us more than we can handle, and thought about how a lighter load would've been nice. No pun intended.

Fortunately, the local Laundromat was only five minutes away and empty. I cleaned the washers with disinfectant wipes, and started my seven loads with no wait. Rather than leave and return for my laundry later, I remained there. On TV, Dr. Oz introduced his featured guest, a doctor who could analyze people's skin and facial shapes to determine whether they had cancer. The word "cancer" piqued my interest. As the segment began, he discussed how specific face shapes and skin colors could show people's health problems. I found his premise hard to believe. I watched half-heartedly, and thought, *Were these signs I missed too?* While I knew that most people found Dr. Oz reputable, I found this segment unbelievable. My disdain for cancer undoubtedly influenced my opinion; however, the last place I thought I'd have to be bombarded by the thought of missed early warning signs was at a Laundromat.

After I'd bagged the wet laundry into trash bags, I returned home to dry it, make dinner, and clean the bathrooms. Before I started on the bathroom floor, I had a coughing fit. Though better, I still started to cough when I tried to do too much. Heeding God's message, I decided the floor would have to wait. Ken told me to rest; he'd said I had too much nervous energy, but it wasn't that. I wanted a clean house before Jill and Ted arrived from Toledo.

My cousin and her husband arrived as I finished my carrots, grapes, and a bagel with peanut butter. My nurse navigator Ellen suggested a sizeable snack since I couldn't eat from midnight until after the surgery. When my cousin showed me the Easter baskets she'd made for the kids, I appropriated some jellybeans from their baskets. We talked awhile, and then we headed to bed.

I had to arrive approximately two hours before my surgery time, now moved to 9 AM, so Ken and I awoke and left before sunrise. As we drove to Columbus, Ken asked how I was. Mentally prepared, I felt calm, with a tinge of sadness but no fear. As for Ken, I didn't know what was in his mind, but I knew he was concerned. Later, I would learn he considered March 1 the longest day of his life.

We entered Mount Carmel Hospital and walked through the maze-like halls to reach the central elevators. We entered, and Ken hit the third-floor button. I was ready. Fortunately, I'd overcome my sinus infection and bronchitis, so I hadn't had to postpone the surgery. At the registration desk, I gave the woman my driver's license and insurance card.

Then a nurse led me to a room. Walking in made it real. It felt like approaching the open casket of a loved one: You knew the person was dead, but to see them was a gut-wrenching verification of mortality. Today, I was going to lose my breasts. The nurse handed me a bag with a gown and slippers, a separate bag for my clothing, and then gave further instructions. I felt the sadness strip away my strength, so I headed for the bathroom with the bag and shut the door. Once again, I was in a room with no tissues! Unrolling toilet paper, I ripped enough to dab my tears. I wanted no evidence. To stay strong, I had to look strong. To remain positive, I needed to readjust my thoughts. Done dressing, I put my clothes in the bag, then took a moment to inhale deeply and reset my mind.

When I opened the door, I saw Ken in the middle of the room. I became mush. My reset failed. For me, tears showed weakness. In solitude, I didn't mind being weak. In public, I did. I moved toward Ken, wrapped my arms around his chest, and laid my head upon it. He hugged me, and assured me I would be fine. He was right, but I didn't want this to be my reality.

Ken spoke of my strength. Part of me wondered if his pep talk was as much for him as for me. There'd been several nights when he couldn't sleep. Not wanting to talk about what he felt, he blamed work. Ken had his code. He couldn't let his worries be mine because he wanted to be my rock, so he hid his fears.

I left Ken's arms and sat in a chair beside my overnight bag. Rather than watch *The Price is Right*, I grabbed Dr. Wayne Dyer's book, *The Power of Intention*, from my bag. Reading it had given me the proper mindset since the day I was diagnosed. His words were my arsenal. I failed more than once to remember what I'd read, and needed to reread. My mind multitasked: I processed Dyer's words, heard Drew Carey's game-show voice and the audience applause, and dwelt on my loss. I strained to prioritize Dyer's words, but I was losing; the score wasn't even close.

Then a nurse diverted my attention. She handed Ken a key to a locker where he could put our belongings and directed him to the waiting room. There he would stay until they'd finished

prepping me for surgery. He took my belongings except for
The Power of Intention. As I held the book, I turned left, and
Ken went right.

I followed the nurse down the hallway to a larger room. As
I entered, I saw the surgery board and noticed that my surgery had changed from 9 AM to 11 AM. There were multiple
cubicles, and she directed me to the last one on the left. I sat
on the stretcher, placed Dyer's book to my left, and lay back.
The nurse closed the curtain to provide privacy. She asked me
some preoperative questions and took my blood pressure and
temperature. Both were fine. Next, she prepared my right hand
for the IV needle. I looked away. I felt a pinch, then saw her put
tape over the tubing to keep the IV in place. Then she proceeded
to attach circular adhesive electrodes, used to monitor heart rate
during surgery, over my chest and back. Then, since the room
was slightly cold, she laid warm blankets over me.

I began to succumb to sadness again, so I opened Dr. Dyer's
book to chapter 4: "Obstacles to Connecting to Intention."
I knew his words would revive my inner strength. If there was
truth to perfect timing, then it came that day. On the last page
of the chapter, I read:

> Good morning, This is God.
> I will be handling
> All of your Problems today.
> I will not need
> Your help, so have
> A miraculous day.

Calm replaced sadness. My smile returned. I giggled softly.
After a silent thank-you, I continued to read. Dr. Dyer wrote
that one "should view obstacles as opportunities to circulate the
power of your unbending intent." He explained to be at peace

meant "detaching yourself from the circumstances, and seeing yourself as the observer rather than the victim… then turning it all over to your Source and knowing that you'll receive the guidance and assistance you require." Advice taken.

Ken returned. I wanted to read more but set the book aside due to my love for him and my concern for his feelings. Ken was nervous for me. Dyer's good-morning words had put me at ease and resurrected my positive spirit. There would be no need for resets. I was ready to face the day.

Dr. Majmudar was the first member of the surgical team to visit me. My nurse asked him to look at my IV. She thought it might have collapsed. I was grateful when he assured her it hadn't. The doctor looked at me with empathy and told me everything would be okay. I agreed, and said that I trusted him and my other doctors completely. I was with the A-Team. When Dr. Majmudar saw what I was reading, he was impressed. He was familiar with Dr. Dyer's works, and spoke highly of him. After we'd discussed our introduction to Dyer's writings and our thoughts about his message, the doctor left.

Taking my IV for a walk, I went to the bathroom. Inside I heard the melodic tones of Brahms' *Lullaby* through the speaker system. During the morning, I'd heard it twice. Why was this song played intermittently? Was it a soothing technique for preoperative patients? A good thought, but when I inquired, the nurse told me it was played each time a baby was born at Mt. Carmel.

At 10 AM I needed an injection of blue dye for the sentinel-node biopsy. A male orderly wheeled my gurney to the room where the doctor would inject me. In the hallway, we learned they'd postponed my operation again. Rather than wheel me back to pre-op, he left me stationed along the wall of a short corridor until it was time to inject the dye.

Dressed only in a gown, I felt out of place while I waited. I'd seen patients in the same predicament during emergency room visits with my children. Now I knew how they felt. Ken and I watched medical staff carry food into a lounge. Having eaten nothing since midnight, I found every aroma delicious. A thoughtful nurse brought me some paparazzi magazines, but they weren't my preferred reading material. I put them on the stretcher, talked with Ken, took a phone call from my Aunt Elaine in New Jersey, and texted a friend who'd left a message.

When it came time, an orderly wheeled me—without Ken—into a small room. The doctor explained the procedure. First, he would inject some radioactive liquid into my left and right breasts. Next, he would inject a dye that would stain the lymph nodes blue. The first auxiliary nodes, called the sentinel nodes, that became blue or radioactive would be removed. Since the MRI had detected no cancer in my lymph nodes, Dr. Sickle-Santanello would remove, dissect, and send only a few sentinel nodes to a pathologist for further analysis. I watched the nurse help prepare the materials. She put two needles on the tray. After I'd been injected, a different orderly wheeled me back to pre-op.

My next visitor was Ellen, my nurse navigator. She held a white kraft-paper bag with handles. It was the gift I hadn't wanted. It surprised Ken, but I knew what was in that bag—GRACE, the stuffed polar bear I first saw in a plexiglass container at the Mount Carmel Imaging Center. Had I donated $25, I'd have partially paid for her, but I hadn't that day because GRACE, a reminder of an undesired outcome, gave me a bad feeling.

Ellen put the bag next to my knees, stood next to Ken, and asked how I was doing. After a brief conversation, she pulled out the bear. I knew GRACE was coming, but I hadn't known her purpose. She wasn't just a stuffed animal; she was part of my recovery.

Ellen showed how to use the bear after surgery. When I rode in the car, I was to place GRACE between the seatbelt and me to protect the surgery site. Then, using my arm, she modeled how to use GRACE to prop my surgical arm so as to increase blood flow to the area. She knew I'd have two surgical arms, so she demonstrated using a pillow to support the other arm. Eventually, she returned GRACE to the bag and handed it to Ken.

Next, Ellen modeled a post-surgery exercise designed to strengthen my arms. I would stand in front of the wall and, with each arm, finger-walk up the wall as far as I could. She suggested I do this exercise ten times twice a day. Also, she gave me post-surgery do's and don'ts, most of which I knew from Dr. Sickle-Santanello.

Ellen left us with GRACE and said she'd follow up with me next week. Now, GRACE was mine and as soft as I imagined her. At our first meeting, GRACE had symbolized cancer to me, but GRACE wasn't cancer or the result of bad karma. GRACE was a gift to aid the healing process and distance me from cancer.

Chapter Eleven

Pay Me Now or Pay Me Later

Trust in the Lord with all your heart, and do not rely on your own insight. In all your ways acknowledge him, and he will make straight your paths.

—Proverbs 3:5-6 (NRSV)

Impatience countered calm. Throughout the day, my surgery time switched like Grand Central Station's arrival and departure board: from 9 AM to 11 AM to 1 PM to 3:30 PM. Other patients left; I remained the lone patient among fewer nurses. Bored and anxious and tired of waiting, I wanted to be in surgery.

In scrubs, Dr. Sickle-Santanello walked over to the side of my gurney and commented on how she heard I'd come into the hospital wearing jeans. She wanted to know if her source was correct. I verified it and explained that they were loose-fitting, and Ken could pull them up so I wouldn't have to exert my arms. With a serious look, she shook her head and looked toward Ken. I felt like a teenager caught doing something her mother forbade. Ken calmed her fears when he told her he'd packed a pair of my sweatpants. Her nod affirmed that he was the sensible decision-maker.

Both had been protective of me throughout my journey so far. It was endearing, but, like Dr. Sickle-Santanello, Ken erred on the side of caution. Rather than try to counter my stubbornness, he'd let me have my way while he packed sweatpants. If I'd thought wearing jeans with my burnt-orange button-down top would be difficult, I wouldn't have worn them. Besides, I wanted to look like a visitor, not a patient, tomorrow. It felt important to me.

Saying, "Pay me now, or pay me later," the doctor reviewed the post-surgical instructions and emphasized that I was to do nothing—no housework, childcare, errands, or lifting. I was to rest and recover. She knew I would struggle to relinquish my daily duties. She inquired who our help would be for the next four weeks, and Ken said he had the first two weeks, his parents the third, and my parents the fourth. After that, we would use Derek's sitters as needed.

Next, she asked if we had any questions. Ken wanted to know the length of my surgery. She said her procedure would last two and a half hours, and Dr. Holland would finish in an hour. Ken could track my surgery using a find number. After she'd completed the double mastectomy and the sentinel-node dissection, Dr. Sickle Santanello would meet Ken in the waiting area to brief him on the surgery and the node-testing results. I was jealous knowing Ken would have the lymph-node analysis results before I did. Perhaps my jealousy was shallow, considering that he'd have over two hours to wait and worry, whereas I would lie unconscious.

Dr. Sickle Santanello reassured us that I would be fine. Having met my surgical team, I agreed and had no reservations. It was evident that each member cared. The doctor said she would see me shortly after Dr. Holland's emergency surgery. I hoped her words proved true.

Administered anesthesia, I was ready. Ken walked alongside my gurney as an orderly wheeled me out of the pre-op room. Ken followed me to the double doors, but couldn't go farther. We kissed. Here the script changed: I failed to say, "I love you." Instead, I replaced it with an optimistic, "I'll see you soon."

Wheeled left into the first operating room, I was stunned. In contrast with every medical drama I'd watched that had dimly lit rooms, the OR was bright and white. The nurses instructed me to move from the gurney to the operating table. I wanted to thank the team but didn't realize how quickly the anesthetic would work. Soon after I'd moved to the table, I was unconscious.

When I awakened some four hours later, I had one question: Were my lymph nodes cancerous? Ken knew. Though groggy, my voice faint, I called for a nurse. When one approached, I asked if I could speak with my husband. She answered that I could after she took my vitals, and then asked if I was a runner. Based on my calves, she thought I was. Since I'd had a bilateral mastectomy and lymph nodes removed, she couldn't use either arm to monitor my blood pressure, so she used my legs. When she removed the cuff, she recorded my pressure and asked if I felt nauseated. I did, so she put a Benadryl patch on my arm. After that, she called the waiting room, asked for Ken, and brought me the phone. I asked Ken about my lymph nodes, and he told me that both were cancer-free. When I asked whether Dr. Sickle Santanello had discussed anything else, he said it could wait until I was in my room. As hard as I tried to pull more information from him, Ken stood firm.

It took longer than expected to reach my room, probably due to fewer staff members, since mine was the last scheduled operation on a Friday evening. In the post-op room, I was the only patient while two nurses cleaned and prepped for the next day. Eventually, someone took me back to the seventh floor.

Impatience for knowledge trumped my hunger pangs. Once settled, I asked Ken about his conversation with Dr. Sickle-Santanello. He figured I'd have forgotten, so he asked what I remembered, then appeared shocked when I reiterated our last conversation. Though groggy from the anesthesia and morphine, I was ready to know how it had gone.

Ken pulled out his notes and proceeded: The surgery went well. Dr. Sickle-Santanello froze three sentinel lymph nodes closest to the left-breast masses, where she would expect the cancer masses to deposit, and three to four more small lymph nodes near the right breast to send for further testing. Results would arrive by midweek. Before my next appointment, in two weeks, I was to drink plenty of fluids to flush out the anesthetic, walk around to help drain fluids, take Oxycodone orally every four to eight hours to avoid the pain, and stay inside the house for the first week. In addition, nurses had to do IVs or blood pressure readings on my right arm. Then, before tomorrow's discharge, the doctor would call me.

Next, I wanted food. After not having eaten for twenty hours, I hoped a hospital meal would've awaited me. To my dismay, that was not the case, and the cafeteria was closed. When my nurse offered me Jell-O and graham crackers, she sensed my disappointment. She suggested the Tim Hortons in the lobby. That might have sounded reasonable, but a donut was a snack, and I yearned for a full-course meal to abate my ravenous hunger. Ken went for food while the nurse brought me a few packets of graham crackers and red gelatin. Famished, I ate it all before Ken returned with only a doughnut. It was a sweet gesture, but it wasn't enough.

Then, restless, I asked my nurse if I could walk around the floor. She said it would be fine. The morphine lessened my pain to a tolerable level, but any arm movement was painful, so I relied on my abdominal muscles, Ken's supportive hand behind my back, and GRACE to help me sit or stand up from a reclined position. As Ken helped me out of bed, I held the metal pole from which my IV fluids hung. It was a slow walk around the wing, but it felt good to be up and moving. I glanced into other rooms and noticed older patients were asleep, talking with visitors, or watching television. I completed a full lap of the hospital wing and discovered that I was the youngest patient. What was wrong with this picture? I didn't belong. While I shouldn't have been shocked, it accentuated how unbelievable this scenario was.

My politeness might have prompted the post-op nurse to inquire about a room more accommodating for Ken, but her efforts were fruitless, most likely due to the lateness of the hour. Ken's six-foot-three stature made the makeshift bed of two wooden chairs uncomfortable. A good night's sleep was important before his increased responsibilities. I told him to go home, sleep, and return in the morning, but he insisted on staying. The caretaker won. We were complementary: I worried about him; he worried about me. Though Ken positioned GRACE, as Ellen had shown us earlier, under my left arm, and laid a folded pillow as an armrest for the right arm, I found it hard to sleep on my back with drains alongside me. In addition, the night nurse disturbed our sleep to check my vitals and empty my drains.

In the morning, I listened eagerly for the wheels of the breakfast cart and watched the glacial pace of the clock until I finally heard the blessed knock on the door. The cafeteria worker entered and put my breakfast tray on the bedside table. I thanked him, then devoured every item on the tray.

My hunger satisfied, I was ready to leave. Discharged by early afternoon, I stripped off the hospital gown and put on real clothes. Dr. Sickle-Santanello encouraged sweatpants, but I wanted to avoid looking like a patient.

When Ken and I arrived home, my cousin, her husband, Ted, and the kids, especially Derek, were happy to see me. Jill and Ted reported that the kids had been well-behaved. As I sat on the couch, Derek lunged to embrace me; Jill pulled him back into her lap with a hug. His face communicated confusion and hurt following repeated attempts. He wanted to hug and kiss me. He looked at GRACE, and his eyes seemed to ask, *Why is a stuffed animal better than me?* Ouch! How to communicate that that wasn't so? I pointed to my chest and told him mommy had a boo-boo, and the polar bear was there to protect it. Derek still wanted to be near me, but he settled for sitting between Jill and me until Jill prepared him for bed. Afterward, Ken and I discussed the surgery with Jill and Ted and thanked them for their help.

My first night home went well. The kids settled into bed. Derek slept without me having to hold, rock, or sing to him. Ken emptied my drains into a specimen cup, measured the bloody mixture in each, recorded the time and amount, and safety pinned them to the mini-hoops on each side of my surgical bra. Ken helped me to bed, adjusted the pillows behind my back, and positioned GRACE and another pillow below each arm. Propped up so I could get out of bed with little pain, I slept well.

In the morning, Jill and Ted returned to Toledo. The transition began.

Chapter Twelve

Exiting Perfect

Better a diamond with a flaw than a pebble without.

—Confucius

The alarm started our Monday. Ken emphasized I rest. No longer in charge, I prayed I'd done enough. I knew my older children were capable and responsible, but I fought sleep. I waited to be needed. The snap of brown paper bags, the refrigerator and freezer doors opening, and the pop of the toaster signaled a seamless transition. I heard no complaints even though the menu had changed from French toast, eggs, sausage, or pancakes to cold cereal, hot cereal, toaster waffles, or Pop-Tarts. I heard the zipping of bookbags, the patter of feet toward the garage door, and the school-bus pulling away; morning one proved successful.

Cancer shifted my life from fast to slow. I relished having no schedule. The luxury of sleep and no responsibilities came at a price, but I celebrated the benefits since the negatives were egregious. I didn't miss rushing from place to place, the working lunches, the absence of silence as I went from the classroom to transportation duties, or ending my day with making dinner and kitchen cleanup. Nonetheless, relaxation proved difficult for me.

Ken checked on me and insisted I rest. By 10 AM my rest-lessness peaked. To reach an upright position without the help of Ken's hand in the middle of my back, I slid my legs over the side of the bed, gripped GRACE in a bear hug over my chest, and used my legs to anchor me while I did a sit-up. Doctors suggested I sleep in a recliner or propped up on the couch for the first few weeks. I wanted my bed, so I built an incline out of three pillows.

Now I needed Ken to strip, clean, and record the fluid level of my drains. He took to it like a soldier. Regimented and meticulous by nature, he emptied the drains at least twice a day. After we'd washed our hands, I unfastened the safety pins that held the drainage bulbs to my surgical bra while Ken lifted the sides to check my drain-line incisions for infection. Seated on the edge of our tub, he gripped the tube closest to the incision, then used his thumb and index finger to strip small tubing sections of fluid and blood to deter blockage. Once he'd pinched where he had left off, he released the tubing. With the tubing stripped, I unscrewed the bulb, whose contents Ken emptied into a pee cup and handed the bulb back to me. Next, he noted the time and measured the fluid levels for each side. I squeezed the air out of the palm-sized, soft plastic bulb, screwed it back on, and released the bulb to restore suction. Finally, Ken poured the contents into the toilet, flushed the fluids, rinsed the pee cup, and disinfected the sink and toilet.

It hurt to raise my arms above my waist and chest, so Ken helped me dress. Pants were easy, but shirts were not. It would've been easier to stay in my nightclothes, but I didn't want to. I wanted to wear jeans and a new button-down shirt. Wearing my recovery nightclothes, baggy sweatpants, and one of Ken's T-shirts made me feel tired and unattractive. On the other hand, dressing up supported my inner strength and positive outlook. I knew my outer appearance would affect how visitors treated me too.

I performed arm exercises before going downstairs. Doing three repetitions with each arm, I walked my fingers gradually up the wall. Pain stopped me when I reached a 120-degree angle. My left arm's mobility was significantly more than my right.

Downstairs, I sat on the couch with GRACE and some reading material. Ken covered me with a blanket, made me something to eat, and ensured that I ate while Derek played on the floor. Groggy due to medication, I slept intermittently between pages or televised storylines while Ken, done with chores for the moment, worked on his laptop. The day was quiet and slow. Our threesome time ended when Aleya came home on the bus. She had a snack, did homework, and readied herself for gymnastics. Trent remained at school for track. Ken took Derek along while on taxi duty; he dropped Aleya off at the YMCA for team practice and picked Trent up from track practice.

As for dinner, my kids' concerns dissipated when Katrina, one of Derek's babysitters, arrived. The smell of her fried chicken, potatoes au gratin, and fresh Italian bread had their mouths watering. As soon as Katrina left, the kids dug into the home-cooked meal. God is good!

Had our family's first-day transition been graded, we'd have made the dean's list with one exception, Derek's nighttime routine. The fault was mine. I should have prepared him for the staff change. Derek was used to Ken or me coming to bathe and change him, brush his teeth, and read him a bedtime story. He waited for me to perform the final goodnight, expecting me to stand next to his crib, hold him in my arms, and rest my head upon his while I swayed back and forth. Derek wanted me to sing to him the bedtime song (sung to the tune of *Frère Jacques*).

Mommy loves you.
Mommy loves you.
Yes, I do.
Yes, I do.
I really, really love you.
Really, really love you.
Yes, I do.
Yes, I do.

He waited and then called, but I never came. Instead, Ken returned, enticing Derek with another book. He enjoyed the story, as Ken used Derek's name instead of the main character's, but the diversion failed. After reading the story, Ken covered him, and Derek, in broken-record fashion, asked for me. I felt sorry; I had done Ken a disservice.

Derek was my last. Greedy, I hadn't transitioned to the final nighttime moment. I should have. A month's sacrifice was small, but I felt robbed of Derek's toddler days, so few and quickly gone. I wanted to pick him up, embrace him, smother him with kisses, and smell the lingering scent of baby lotion on his skin while I rocked him to sleep.

Between breaths and sobs, Derek called for me. Each shriek, retribution for my selfishness, pained my heart. I wanted to comfort him, but I knew walking into his room would exacerbate the situation. Patiently, Ken soothed him. Once asleep, Derek relapsed into a newborn's sleep pattern, waking every two to four hours. Even after Ken entered his room and told him I was asleep, he asked for me repeatedly.

At the start of the week, my transition scores were less than stellar in medication advice and bathing. The observation-room nurse had warned that failure to take pain medication on time would result in extreme discomfort until the medicine took effect, but I failed to heed her advice. When my pain subsided,

I stretched the period between Oxycontin pills, which led to distress for several hours. Bathing, an emotional hurdle, meant I'd see my chest breastless. Strong as I had grown, I feared that sight would relapse me into a depressive state. I was scheduled to see Dr. Holland on Friday and knew a bath was inevitable; however, I evaded it until Tuesday.

Dr. Holland and Dr. Sickle-Santanello held different views on bathing. Dr. Holland said showering was fine, but Dr. Sickle-Santanello suggested sponge baths until after the drain removal. I preferred Dr. Holland's opinion because a sponge bath meant Ken would have to look at me, but I listened to Dr. Sickle-Santanello.

While Ken waited outside the bathroom, I undressed. I gritted my teeth as my fingers gingerly undid the hook and eyes of my surgical bra. I didn't know what was more painful, undoing my bra or seeing what it concealed. Upon the iodine-yellowed canvas of my once virgin skin, I saw horror. The smooth, clean skin that bordered the image heightened its hideousness. Looking at the mutilation, I felt like a Van Gogh self-portrait. The dark and somber color palette, compliments of surgical bruising, mixed black, purple, and blue, which conveyed my feelings. The brush strokes were splotchy and irregular in size. Jagged diagonal lines of stitches crossed my chest, and the absence of nipples left me aghast. Nasty. I was nasty. If titled, the work would have been *Anger Meets Disgust*. Now, my chest, no longer art, reminded me of what cancer had taken. I felt like damaged goods, and wondered, *Could I ever look beautiful again?*

Gawking at my horror, I stood frozen. Cold and naked, I tried to compose myself like I had in the hospital bathroom. I thought *Don't cry! Stay strong! Erase the image! You are beautiful!*

Who was I kidding? Minus the bruises, this wasn't temporary; it was permanent. My breasts were gone! My tits, my sexual starters, gone! My breasts and their sense of sensation were never coming back, and to let Ken in to see me like this? No way! This image couldn't replace the one he knew.

When I got married and my initials changed, my dad told me that Ken turned me into a "gem." Now looking at my mucked up and defaced chest, I thought, *So much for being Ken's gem.* Externally flawed, my chest blemished my gem's clarity. While it is said a person's internal self matters more than one's external appearance, that adage fell short of consoling me amid my visual reality.

I grabbed a hand towel, covered the mess, stood in the tub, and called for him. He entered, took a washcloth from the linen closet, turned the faucet to warm, and began to lather the washcloth. Gentle and quick, he washed my body. I shivered, whether due to exposure to the cold air or my horror, I didn't know. An awkward silence accompanied us. Ken sensed my inner discomfort, and I felt his pain for me. Finished, he wrapped me in a towel and dried me, then stepped outside the bathroom so I could put on my bra. He'd have asked if I needed help, but he understood. I dropped the hand towel that had concealed my disfigurement onto the sink and grabbed my clean surgical bra. Scarring, a constant reminder, ruptured my self-image. In the mirror, I took one last look before the bra, like a bandage, hid my marred chest.

By Wednesday I was on an upswing. The grogginess faded, and restlessness bordered irritability. My recovery started to feel more like house arrest. During a call, my mother laughed, marveling at how I had made it three days. As Ken did my roles and his own, I wanted to help, but I heard a little voice say, "Pay me now or pay me later," and knew Dr. Sickle-Santanello had foreseen this. She was the angel on my shoulder, opposite my devil's conscience, the one trying to have me play superhero.

Meals kept coming, whether home cooked, takeout, or purchased with gift cards. Victoria's meat lasagna, salad, and garlic bread, my fifth-grade colleagues' noodle casserole and Kentucky Fried Chicken and green bean casserole, as well as the fourth-grade teachers' treat of Bob Evans, followed by the second-grade teachers' gift card for Domino's pizza, were all much appreciated. Due to their generosity, my husband, kids, and I ate nourishing, well-balanced meals. Even after ample portions, there were leftovers.

Wednesday night, we solved Derek's nighttime transition. First, when we put him in the crib, Ken said goodnight as I sat next to the crib. Then, worried about my comfort, Ken put a pillow against the wall behind me and laid a blanket over me. Through the slats, Derek kissed and hugged me. Finally, he lay down, turned his head, and watched as I sang until he fell asleep.

Thursday's sponge bath wasn't as emotionally traumatizing as Tuesday's. The shock had begun to wear away, and I saw the dark, angry mess as my fighting bruises. I still wasn't ready to show Ken, but I could at least look at myself in the mirror without crying. It was also less painful to undo the hooks and eyes of my surgical bra.

Finally, my house arrest ended Friday morning with a car ride to see Dr. Holland. His nurse suggested removal of my surgical drains. I declined and decided to exercise caution. The left and right bulb drainage had to be 20mL or less twenty-four hours before removal. I looked forward to being drain free, but preferred to wait to remove them. My right and left bulb drainage was on the cusp of 20mL or less, so I knew Dr. Sickle-Santanello would advise me to keep them longer. Afterward, Dr. Holland examined the surgery site. Since the area was healing nicely, I was allowed to leave the house and begin walking. As for running, not that I felt able, I had to wait another three weeks.

On our return home, Ken, Derek, and I celebrated with a walk. Ken pushed the jogging stroller, and Derek, who enjoyed my running pace, requested he go faster. I, however, moved like a tortoise. My chest felt foreign with each stride. Patient with my slower pace, Ken asked if I wanted to turn around after a half-mile. I chose to walk a mile, but my stubbornness cost me: The following day, I felt sick and weak. I had done too much. I needed to learn that I couldn't sprint out of the gate. It would take my body time to be ready for my usual pace. The next evening, I made the right decision, scaled the distance back to a half-mile, and felt better the next day.

Life was not about racing or flawlessness. As a mom, wife, and teacher, it was hard to try to manage everything, but I needed to shed the superhero cape and stop chasing life. I needed to prioritize and start learning how to appreciate the art of walking. Stop trying to make days longer than twenty-four hours. Stop seeking perfection, from raising kids to household chores to teaching. My pace, not my goals, had to be reset. I needed to stop trying to build Rome in a day, accept I could not, and drop the sense of inadequacy that accompanied it. Sometimes, I had to put myself first, a hard act, as much as it should be easy. If I didn't stand up for my needs, I could forget about anyone doing it for me. It was like waiting for a train when the last one had already left the station. Most of all, I needed to embrace my scars and imperfections, knowing I was a child of God, created in His image.

Chapter Thirteen

Still Smiling

Keep your face always toward the sunshine and shadows will fall behind you.

—Walt Whitman

Uncertainty became my extended company, as the pathology results would determine additional treatment. I knew cancer had stages, but I was unaware that other characteristics, such as lymph-node status, tumor size, estrogen and progesterone status, and human epidermal growth factor receptor 2 (HER2), affected breast-cancer treatment plans. If I were estrogen and progesterone positive, meaning cancer cells grew in response to the hormones, then the hormonal therapy Tamoxifen would be prescribed. HER2-positive cancer, one more likely to come back, grow faster, and spread, would require chemotherapy. My ultrasound scans showed my tumor sizes at 1.5 cm or less, and my sentinel lymph-node biopsy found no cancerous nodes, so radiation seemed highly unlikely.

Dr. Sickle-Santanello's nurse practitioner, Suzanne Robertson, called on Monday morning. When she said that my pathology results were optimal, I was elated. My lymph nodes, right breast tissue, and margins, the tissues around the tumors, were cancer free. My tumors tested estrogen and progesterone positive. Initially, the HER2 was indeterminate.

Further analysis found I was HER2 negative, so an additional test, called Oncotype DX, was needed using tissue from my tumors. During a period of seven to ten days, a pathologist would analyze twenty-one genes that affected how cancer would likely behave and respond to treatment. A recurrence score—low (below 18), intermediate (18–30), or high (31–100)—would determine whether chemotherapy outweighed the risk of its side effects. With an intermediate to high recurrence score, I'd need chemotherapy. With my tumor tissue on its way to California, I was again in a holding pattern.

Four days after my conversation with Suzanne, I met with Dr. Sickle-Santanello. In the examination room, she acknowledged, without surprise, my disposition with the phrase "And you're still smiling."

First, I named the positive events: my drains coming out tomorrow, using my left arm fully, and near-full mobility of the right. Then I told her that Dr. Holland's nurse had wanted to remove the drains last Thursday, but I thought it was too soon.

She smiled as I restated, "'Pay me now, or pay me later,' right?" She winked at me and sat on her stool.

My mind was on chemotherapy. Its potential side effects didn't matter because I wanted to be aggressive. A missed cancer cell was a dangerous seed. When I asked, Dr. Sickle-Santanello redirected the conversation. I pushed. She stood firm. Due to being estrogen and progesterone positive, HER2 negative, and having cancer-free lymph nodes, my treatment plan was on hold until the surgery site healed and my oncotype scores arrived. While Ken breathed a sigh of relief, I curbed my impatience with thoughts of tomorrow's drain removal.

The next day, we sat in Dr. Holland's waiting room. I read while Ken responded to emails. At the end of a chapter,

I reflected on how well Ken and I had managed my drains. We experienced only one hiccup, a blockage between the piping and the bulb. Unfortunately, it required a late-night call to Dr. Holland's after-hours number, which neither of us wanted to make. Ken wanted me to remove the piping from the bulb stem, but I worried it would affect the device. It turned out Ken was right. Dr. Holland agreed it would cause no harm and walked us through the steps. First, Ken removed the piping from the bulb screw top and stripped the piping. Then, I pinched the piping where he left off, and Ken ran water through the top screw cap of the bulb. After removing the blockage, he put the piping back and screwed it on the bulb top. Again, we worked well as a team.

Ken looked up from his phone, caught my stare, and asked why I was smiling. I replied, "I'd rather be the sun than the rain." He smiled and returned to his emails. I resumed reading. His question distracted me, however; it brought to mind others who'd questioned my happiness in times of struggle. My high-school guidance counselor wondered how I could smile as I told her about my dad's layoff due to a business merger, and the financial straits that then influenced my college choices. My upbeat attitude while facing cancer stunned my teaching colleagues. Yesterday, Dr. Sickle-Santanello had greeted me with "And you're still smiling."

Life is influenced by choice, attitude, and circumstance, but it doesn't stop unless one lets it. Along one's path, rain and sunshine occur. Tears of consequence and hardship bring growth, while constant downpours usher destruction. Happiness, however, generates light. My smile, a signal of my mindset, was my heart.

A nurse opened the door and called my name. I knew Ken would rather not see the drain removal, so I offered to go alone. Ken asked whether I minded. While I felt a little anxious, I didn't mind. I wondered if I'd feel any pain even though I had taken a pain pill an hour earlier. The nurse took me into the first room and left me with a paper gown. When she returned, she asked me to lie on the table. As she removed the tubing from the right-side drain, I took a deep breath and slowly exhaled as instructed. I felt only a slight sensation. The length of the tubing surprised me because I was unaware that the tubing started in the armpit and circumnavigated the expansion implant. After the nurse had removed the left-side tube I was free to go.

As I left the office, I could have skipped to the car. Yes, there was possible chemotherapy and further reconstruction. As two weeks after surgery neared a close, however, I celebrated the small victories! My drains were gone, the incisions were healing nicely, and my soreness was minimal. My walking distance and speed increased, and my arm movement improved!

As for my family, they survived the transitions and adaptations, and made my recovery journey more manageable. Ken's caretaker shift and absence from the office ended as our parents were on deck. My two older children's lives were minimally affected even without me at the helm. Trent went to his track practices and meets and continued to volunteer every other Saturday with Mrs. Schafer, a local photographer, and her daughter at the local Humane Society. At the same time, Aleya made all team practices to prepare for Districts. With the drains removed, I had intended to go to her meet, but Ken, like Dr. Sickle-Santanello, decreed a protective no. Afraid I was pushing too hard too soon, he felt the four-hour round-trip drive, the three-to-four-hour competition, and the award ceremony would be too fatiguing. Though late, I had planned and sent invitations for Aleya's birthday party. Affected most, Derek regressed to waking multiple times in the night, screaming for me, which made Ken set up the pack-and-play next to our bed. It worked well, so we decided to keep Derek in it until I could hold him.

In addition, family, friends, colleagues, and people I had never met made the first two recovery weeks a success. Ken's job would have been much harder without their generous meal donations and time. The cards and various care packages were uplifting delights, and the prayer commitment to my family and me was overwhelming. Going into the third week, I thought their spoiling me would subside. I was wrong.

The following morning, I noticed an envelope in the mail with AnnMarie's name on the return address label. How wonderful! In addition to taking my calls and answering my emails, she'd sent me a letter too. I expected an inspirational message or advice. What I found moved me. As I opened the card, a piece of paper fell to the kitchen floor. It was a check. A look at the amount made my eyelids brim with tears. In gratitude, I said Wow! three times. Once the shock subsided, I read AnnMarie's message.

> Dear Gwyn,
> Please know your Brunner Family is thinking of you and wants to help, so we decided to take up a collection. You can use this money for babysitting, takeout, or anything you need or want. We all love and care for you.
>
> You are amazing and so positive! Keep up the fight. Please know that you are always in our thoughts.
>
> All our love and prayers,
> Your Brunner Family
> xoxoxo

The closing, Your Brunner Family, touched me. Though I'd received cards and emails from retired and current staff, I never expected them to take up a collection for me. The Brunner Elementary School staff, a close unit, cared about each other as much as about their students. Though absent from Scotch Plains, New Jersey, and my Brunner family for two years, I was still considered a family member. Their care, love, support, generosity, and prayers pulled at my heartstrings.

When I was little, angels had wings. Found on beautiful stained-glass windows and painted murals, Michael and Gabriel, God's messengers, were ethereal. Now, my angels, people close and unknown, were mortal, visible, and abundant. They held my hands without physicality. They supported my family and me, and cheered us from the sidelines as we faced cancer and all its challenges. My earthly angels' extremely generous pampering humbled me. To each of these angels I was grateful beyond words. When the cup of love pours down on you, it brings a warm and everlasting strength.

Chapter Fourteen

The Green Light

Giving up will never get you to the finish line. You've got to just keep going.

—Mary Bryant

My dream to run my third Columbus Marathon lingered. Dr. Sickle-Santanello, my parents, and my husband said no, but telling me, the stubborn, determined one that I couldn't do something only fueled my desire. While they wanted the pot off the stove, I kept it simmering on the back burner.

I felt fine and more energetic with each passing day, and was already planning my first run, though I was careful not to push myself too fast. I had during the second week, but I'd learned to listen to my body. I yearned to increase my daily mileage and pace, and was elated and proud when I reached four miles by week three. Though tempted to run during week four, I kept my pace brisk, topped off at a level of speed walking. I no longer felt like the tortoise; I was ready to be the hare.

As I talked with my parents in the family room, I heard my cell phone. I saw the words "Surgical Oncology" and knew Suzanne was calling with my breast cancer gene results. I took the phone into the study for privacy and answered. My oncotype scores, 26 and 28, placed me at the high end of the intermediate risk of recurrence; chemotherapy was therefore necessary.

After I'd discussed what was next with Suzanne, I chose not to tell my parents. I didn't want chemotherapy to plague their visit with me; however, I did call Ken, who was away on a business trip. While I hadn't allowed myself to foresee an early exit, Ken had, and I knew he'd be troubled by the news. He told me to call when I knew. When he heard the news, he said, "I feel like we've been hit in the gut again."

Later that night, I delved into data-collection mode while I sat beside Derek's crib to lull him to sleep. I sought advice from AnnMarie via email and reliable internet sites such as Susan G. Komen, Mayo Clinic, Cancer Research UK, and YSC (Young Survival Coalition). Inundated with questions, and unwilling to wait until my medical oncologist appointment, I sought answers. With AnnMarie, my questions were patient related. What chemo drugs did you receive? Did you experience nausea, fatigue, weight gain, mouth sores, or chemo brain? How long did the symptoms last? After treatments, how long did it take for your hair to grow back? Did your eyebrows and eyelashes fall out? If so, did your eyes become irritated? On the Web, I read about chemotherapy drugs. A few side effects of breast cancer chemo drugs included leukemia, but Doxorubicin, Epirubicin, and Trastuzumab could affect the heart. On the YSC website, I clicked on SURVIVOR STORIES, read the bios of stage-1 women near my age, and took notes on how they handled their treatments and difficulties.

As I scrolled through the bios, I came to a survivor named Mary Bryant. I'd been at a red light for a fall marathon due to others' concerns, but I lifted off the brake when I read, "Six days after her fifth round of chemotherapy, Mary Bryant finished her fourth marathon." This Ford model's story changed the red light to green. The pot was back on the front burner! If Mary

Bryant, a marathoner and breast cancer patient at thirty-six, could do it, so could I.

Mary's motto took me back to a childhood lesson from Watty Piper's book, *The Little Engine That Could*. For me, she was the little blue engine. Her story, a determined and inspirational one, mirrored what I sought to do. People like my husband and Dr. Sickle-Santanello told me it wasn't possible; Mary just proved it was. I never let the marathon go because I was confident I could do it. Due to Mary's feat, now I knew I would. Let the training begin!

Chapter Fifteen

End of the Beginning

Nothing in life is to be feared. It is only to be understood.

—Marie Curie

When I walked into the Adena Cancer Center with my two oldest children, I was in the final half of my medical marathon. Given the names of three highly qualified medical oncologists, two in Columbus and one in Chillicothe, I chose the local Dr. Jeffrey VanDeusen. I met him and his family at a fall block party when they moved into our neighborhood. Afterward, we saw each other in passing, and our conversations were brief. My last encounter with him was helping a fallen female biker with multiple skin abrasions and cuts. Our meeting would therefore be an awkward surprise. While the doctor would know me by sight, I was sure he wouldn't recognize my name.

Called back by a nurse, I left the kids in the waiting area. Ken was out of town on business, and wanted me to change my consultation to a date he could make. Dr. VanDeusen was overbooked, and his next appointment was weeks away. I understood Ken's request, but I wanted to start treatment sooner rather than later.

After the nurse had taken my weight and blood pressure, she led me to an exam room and handed me a gown. I declined. Our first meeting wouldn't start with me in a gown. The nurse left. I waited. I heard footsteps and watched the door open. His mouth agape, Dr. VanDeusen looked at me in utter disbelief. I commented on the obvious, how surprised he was to see me. Though the address was familiar, he was unaware it was I. Still stunned, he asked if I was okay with him being my doctor. I responded that I was, as long as he was okay with my being his patient. The awkwardness resolved, Jeff shut the door, took a seat, and the discussion began.

As with a newly learned foreign language, I understood a few words but failed to grasp quite all of them. Though my ears heard Dr. VanDeusen discuss the difference between the chemotherapy medications Adriamycin Cyclophosphamide (AC) and Taxotere Cyclophosphamide (TC), and recent study findings, I was lost. Fortunately, my questions and his explanations helped offset my lack of familiarity with medical terminology. For example, due to my young age, he suggested TC, since AC could harm the heart, and recent research data proved TC was as effective as AC if not more so. When I heard six months, however, I wanted to cry because Dr. Sickle-Santanello had mentioned a treatment timeline of two to three months. When I questioned the length, I found I had misunderstood again.

Then we progressed to the prescriptions, and as Dr. Van-Deusen rattled off the medications and their purpose, I thought *My body is about to become a pharmacy!* First, there was dexamethasone (Decadron)—a steroid with the potential side effects of increased appetite, insomnia, fluid retention, and extra sensitivity to the sun's rays—which I had to take the morning and night before chemotherapy as well as the two mornings afterward. Next, I had to take omeprazole (Prilosec) before breakfast and dinner for three to four days after chemo to prevent nausea and vomiting. Prochlorperazine (Compazine) was necessary once I felt the onset of nausea; if I failed to take it soon enough, it would take a while to work. Next, there was stomatitis mixture, or Magic Mouthwash, to swish and swallow for sore throat and mouth sores. Dr. VanDeusen decided not to write me a prescription for diarrhea and constipation medication until needed.

Inundated with more prescriptions than I'd ever needed, I reminisced about how much I hated taking medicine. In first grade, I dumped my small salad-dressing holder of strep-throat medication in the corner of the playground until aides spotted me doing it. When I spiked a sudden high fever during a sleepover at my grandparents', I vehemently refused to take the fever reducer my grandfather bought for me. As an adult, I refused to take aspirin or ibuprofen for headaches unless the pain became excruciating or lasted beyond several hours. After the mastectomy, the attending nurse warned me not to stop or stretch my pain medication. It was like she knew me!

No medication, however, would prevent hair loss. Told I would lose hair within three weeks of my first treatment, I planned to keep it until the first massive amount came loose. Then, I would shave it, but I intended to take my youngest, Derek, to the salon to avoid startling him. Though the cancer center's boutique offered breast-cancer patients free wigs, compliments of the Susan G. Komen Foundation, I felt that hats would be more comfortable as we headed into summer. Nonetheless, I entertained the thought of trying one.

Next, I wanted to discuss Neulasta, the shot needed to stimulate my white blood cells after chemo treatment. Having read other breast cancer patients' blogs, I noted that the adverse side effects most often mentioned were severe bone and joint pain, but one patient said that taking Claritin the day before, the day of, and the day after the shot could prevent or alleviate the pain. When Dr. VanDeusen affirmed that, I added yet another drug to my list.

To finish as soon as possible, I chose Friday, April 12. I would receive the chemo intravenously because a port was too invasive, and a PICC line was impossible due to my double mastectomy. Four treatments, twenty-one days apart, would be completed by mid-June, allowing me time to enjoy the summer, travel out of state, have my reconstructive surgery by the end of July, and have enough recuperation time before the start of the 2013–2014 school year. Based on information from YSC blogs and Dr. VanDeusen, I knew the most brutal period would be seven to ten days after treatment. Ken would be home on the weekends, and I knew he could help me through this stretch if I scheduled the treatments on Fridays.

Thinking about Mary Bryant's accomplishment and my naysayers, I asked Dr. VanDeusen about exercise and its intensity during chemotherapy. He cited recent studies that proved exercise beneficial rather than detrimental to cancer patients. A University of North Carolina-Chapel Hill study on rats showed that exercise slowed and reduced the growth of tumors. Another study found positive results when breast-cancer patients ran on treadmills following chemo treatments. Asked if one could exercise too much, the doctor said no; moreover, he told me that exercise could reduce the feeling of fatigue. My can-do spirit roared. Like an ocean tide, the naysayers' qualms went out, and motivation came crashing back. Finally, someone other than me believed Columbus was attainable this fall.

When I returned to the waiting area, my two older kids were alone. The cancer center was closed. Our consultation had taken an hour and a half. When he saw Aleya asleep in a chair, Dr. VanDeusen lightly touched her shoulder. She woke, looking unsettled and confused. I assured her it was all right and helped her gather her books. The doctor walked us to the exit, and told me this was the beginning of the end of my treatment. I saw it differently. Chemotherapy was not the beginning of an end; it was the end of my beginning.

I met with Dr. Holland the next day. Since my diagnosis, doctor's appointments had gone from bimonthly to weekly or daily. My life revolved from one appointment to the next. While the reminder cards had been working well, I might need a calendar on my refrigerator. When I told Ken I wasn't used to having so many doctor's appointments, he pointed out that I had never had cancer.

After another expander fill and examination of my surgical site, Dr. Holland permitted me to run; he suggested I start slowly and gradually increase the mileage as I felt comfortable. The next week, I ran every day, sometimes alone, other times with Derek in the baby jogger. I started the run with a slow one-mile jog. During the first half-mile, my new chest felt awkward and unnatural, a reminder that I wasn't a hundred percent real flesh anymore. As I began to feel stronger, I increased my pace. By the week's end, I logged a five-miler. That felt great, but my biggest accomplishment was a Rocky-atop-the-Philadelphia-Museum-steps moment: I ran up Yaples Orchard Hill, a very steep incline, without a stop. It brought such exhilaration that, cornball enough to reenact the Rocky scene, I did it twice.

In addition to running, I began to research what foods to eat during chemo and stockpile water. I drank two to three liters daily, especially the day before, the day of, and the day after chemo. High-fiber foods were also recommended; there were certain foods to avoid and others that would help me manage symptoms. As I worked to prepare my pantry and refrigerator with such helpful items, I suffered another what-if moment.

My weekly shopping routine never included sweets. Nonetheless, seized by an urge for a confectionery treat, I steered my cart into this aisle. I browsed the shelves and contemplated grabbing gummy bears, Swedish Fish, Milk Duds, Good & Plenty, or my favorite European white chocolate. Then, as quickly as the idea of luxurious indulgence had come, a twinge of betrayal shot back and extinguished my delight with one thought: *Had my occasional sweet-tooth pleasures brought breast cancer my way?*

I left the sweets aisle and entered another, but I didn't want to shop anymore. Sadness blanketed my mood. I began to perceive food as an enemy. Had any of these processed, sugar-laden, hormone-injected, or pesticide-polluted foods led to my diagnosis? The roulette wheel spun, compelling me to search for the cause of my disease. When would I learn to walk away?

Later that evening, my father called. He passed along news of a study he'd heard on the nightly news. The study found that a diet high in animal fats, such as milk, cheese, and ice cream, was linked to breast cancer due to hormones, other growth factors, antibiotics, and pesticides possibly contained in the products. Stop! I knew my father meant well in passing the information, but I didn't want to know. I wasn't trying to hide my head in the sand, but I struggled to eat without reservations or fear, and now I had to include dairy!

After our conversation ended, I wanted to scream. *What can I eat? What won't put me at risk for a cancer recurrence?* Then I thought of my grandfather, who'd eaten a high-fat, cholesterol-laden breakfast of eggs and bacon every morning, and loved his Entenmann's coffee cake and Danish rings. When my aunts, uncle, and father tried to change his eating habits, he wouldn't listen. I remember his adamant declaration that he'd enjoyed this breakfast for over fifty years and was not about to change. If this breakfast was going to kill him, then so be it. Eventually, something kills us, but he would die a happy man. Why couldn't I have the same grit? Was it because I was only forty, with three young kids, the youngest only two, while Grandpa was in his eighties?

The week progressed, and I questioned my food choices every day. I knew I needed to eat to maintain my strength, but I feared eating. I was in a funk. I hoped chemo class would revive my fighter mentality and eliminate the fear that had started to invade me.

Before my first chemotherapy session on Friday, I needed to attend a chemotherapy education class. While very informative, the class made me feel like a college student receiving a syllabus and suggested reading list for the upcoming twelve-week session. My reading material consisted of a cancer cookbook, Dr. Jean E. Sprengel's chemotherapy care book, the *ChemoCompanion Care Guide*, based on one woman's experience of her sister's cancer ordeal, and three large packets that discussed side effects, nutrition, safety precautions, and information for the caregiver. I lugged the armful of material out to my car, but knew that reading multiple sheets of paper in search of answers wouldn't be practical for Ken or me.

I needed to be proactive rather than reactive, so I condensed my reading material into a flipchart for simplicity and quick access. First, since each symptom had at least three pages of information, I separated the packets, grouped pages accordingly, skimmed, highlighted essential facts, and crossed out duplicated ones. Then, using Word, I created a chart for each side effect: constipation, diarrhea, dry mouth, fatigue, hair loss, nausea, and nail and skin changes. Most of my charts had three columns labeled AVOID, MANAGE, and SAFETY ISSUES, and a box below that highlighted conditions that would require me to seek medical attention. Then I made a card for infection signs, safety precautions: 48 hours after chemotherapy, and Taxotere reaction signs. I finished within two days. During a check-up call, Ellen, my nurse navigator, noted that my project sounded marketable. For me, it was an essential item.

Next, I needed to address my mini-pharmacy. To ensure that I'd make no errors, I listed the name, purpose, and dosage of each medication on an index card, then taped the card inside the door of the cupboard where I kept the drugs, along with a recording chart to avoid having to count pills.

Having read the safety precautions, I knew bodily fluids had to be handled carefully for forty-eight hours after chemotherapy. If I became sick, Ken needed to wear gloves and put any clothing or bedding with bodily fluid in a garbage bag until we could wash it. I made three sick bags; each contained one drawstring garbage bag, two disposable latex medical gloves, and an antibacterial wipe. I put one in the top drawer of Ken's nightstand, one in the master bathroom, and one in the main-floor bathroom. Next, I lined all the trashcans and put one near my side of the bed. Later, I gave Ken a tutorial.

Finally, I prepared my chemo bag. In it, I put an educational journal, two videos, snacks, a fleece blanket, a sweatshirt, saltines, mints, several water bottles, and the chemo binder with my flipchart and Taxotere reaction card. With a day to spare, I'd completed my research, prepared my house, and packed my bag.

Like the daunting, mentally and physically fatiguing, and painful final miles of a marathon, chemotherapy would be more challenging than surgery. Therefore, I decided to name my treatment weeks as mile markers. Friday would start mile 14. Outside hair loss, vomiting was the effect I wished to avoid most. Ultimately, the finish would be worth the outcome, my peace of mind.

Chapter Sixteen

Stay Strong

I hereby command you: Be strong and courageous; do not be frightened or dismayed,
for the Lord your God is with you wherever you go.

—Joshua 1:9 (NRSV)

As I entered Adena Cancer Center, I looked like I was going on an overnight trip. After registration, I walked to the chemo unit. Some rooms were off to the left side of the wing entrance for gurney patients. To the right, there were four sheet-covered chairs. With no dividers between the stations, patients could see staff at all times and converse with fellow patients. Each station had a table and an IV stand with machines, and all the chairs faced a wall of plate glass windows. Natural sunlight radiated in, bringing an element of hospitable comfort. The environment didn't feel clinical; it was warm, bright, and inviting.

While visitors' backs faced the windows, patients faced a soon-to-be garden. The architects sought to bring the outside in to the patients. While somewhat an empty canvas, I envisioned its future beauty. Landscaping rocks defined perimeters and paths. Freshly tilled soil awaited foliage and flowers to add color and dimension, and a grass-covered hill accented by a baby-blue sky served as the backdrop.

The ceiling tiles painted by either patients or family members provided inspirational quotes and soothing pictures of nature, animals, symbols, or cancer ribbons. Some quotes were Bible based, while others were letter-like messages or author-inspired text. Though some were dated and dedicated to specific patients, most were for all. These personal touches were uplifting.

I put my chemo bag on the table, sat down, and rolled up my right sleeve. My nurse, Diane, explained what she was doing as she hung my medication bags on the stand. Adept at putting in an IV, she caused me only the pinch of a needle prick. She would inject some medications into my IV by needle, and I'd receive others through the slow drip of an IV bag. Benadryl, the first drug administered, made patients either tired, wired, or ravenous.

An hour later, hunger pangs seized me. My breakfast, a bowl of cereal, proved insufficient, and the saltines and mints, snacks suggested by the chemo literature, wouldn't appease my hunger. I needed more, and regretted having turned down a volunteer's earlier offer of snacks. I asked Diane what snacks were available, and I chose pretzels and a Rice Krispie treat, but my hunger still raged.

Next, Diane offered me various sandwich and soup choices from the main lobby's small cafeteria. I chose a chicken salad croissant sandwich. The portion size was so generous that I should've been able to eat only about half, but I ate the whole sandwich before my hunger subsided.

When Diane started the chemo drugs, I began to drink water, hoping to counteract the potentially harsh effects the Cytoxan, could have on my bladder. Cytoxan tended to stay in the lining of the bladder. I thought water would help flush the medications from my system, so I drank bottle after bottle until I'd drunk all six of the sixteen-ounce bottles I had in my bag. This caused a few trips to the bathroom. After I finished each bottle, I put it in my bag to recycle later.

As a mom and a teacher, I found personal time a rarity. With four hours free of responsibilities, I wanted to relax, but the leisure reading I'd brought was an educational journal. Relaxation was a foreign word to me. I constantly felt like I should be doing something productive, so I treated rest like a waste of time. Next time, I'd put a leisure reading book or magazine in my chemo bag.

While four hours sounded like a long time, the hours moved quickly. Soon, Diane changed the empty chemo bag to a fluid flush, which flushed the chemo medicine out of my veins. After a half hour, Diane removed the IV and I was allowed to leave. Seated in the chemo waiting area by the window, I saw Ken's car enter the parking lot. I made my way to the main lobby and out the door. As Ken drove me home, he said he'd pick up Derek from Katrina, the sitter, on his way home from work.

I felt fine four hours after that first chemo treatment. I wanted to take advantage of the beautiful day and decided to run. An active person, I wasn't used to sitting for several hours. I knew that Derek liked to join me on my runs, so I decided to pick him up early from Katrina's. Once we arrived home, I put him in the stroller and ran three miles. He enjoyed the run as much as I did.

With no signs of fatigue or chemotherapy side effects over the weekend, I wanted to knock on wood in hopes it would continue. On Monday, however, the male nurse who'd given me my first Neulasta shot, which was quick and painless, mentioned that I might experience an achy feeling in a few days. Aware of the side effects, I hoped taking Claritin as advised would mitigate any discomfort.

I returned home and turned on the TV to find out who'd won the Boston Marathon. Instead of seeing runners cross the finish line, I saw the words "Special Report" at the bottom of the screen, images of injured spectators and runners, a finish line covered in debris, and people assisting the injured. Numb, I wanted to console the families who were there to cheer their runners, and comfort those who'd had their special moment derailed by terrorists. As I listened to the news reporters detail the bombing, I thought *This won't stop me from running marathons or Boston when I qualify.*

The phone rang, breaking my trance. It was my mother. I knew what she would say. She asked if I'd seen the news about Boston. After my yes, she questioned whether I should participate in the Columbus Marathon. While I appreciated her concern, she should have known that it would fall on deaf ears. As a cancer patient, I was even more motivated to live life and fear nothing. Evil existed in the world, but my life wouldn't come to a halt. Terrorism notwithstanding, my passion to run a marathon remained steadfast. Columbus was happening.

When I ran the next day, I thought about Boston. I knew that shaving another twenty minutes off of my personal best was a tall order, and the treatments and reconstruction operation would affect my training schedule. However, I wanted it. A surge of emotion caused tears to swell in my lower lids. Whether I qualified for Boston or not, I would continue running for my will was mighty.

Chapter Seventeen

Run, Mommy, Run!

I can do all things through him who strengthens me.

—Philippians 4:13 (NRSV)

Focused on isolation as I entered a low state on Friday, I forgot about my lab appointment. When I remembered, it was too late; the cancer center was closed. I wondered whether I was in trouble, so I dialed Dr. VanDeusen's cell. Not used to so many doctor's appointments, I needed a better system than the appointment reminder cards in my wallet or on the refrigerator. The doctor assured me it was fine. Someone could draw my blood before our Monday morning appointment, but we would have to review my hemoglobin, white, and red blood-cell counts later.

On Monday, as I waited for the nurse to draw my blood into multiple vials, I saw a younger nurse stop and look back. Her look, which consisted of a tilted head, sad eyes, a downturned mouth, and slightly limp shoulders, verified my minority status among an elder majority. I felt like saying, "Your eyes aren't deceiving you. I'm young, and I have breast cancer."

I broke eye contact and turned away, but still felt the nurse's look. It failed to consider who I was, and classified me as a lost cause. My happy and confident demeanor didn't matter. Working in a cancer center, she saw cancer as a death sentence. To her, the Grim Reaper was sucking my life away and leading me to the underworld. Cancer was some people's exit in life, but cancer was different for everyone.

Negative perceptions hovered over cancer patients like black cloaks of can't do. Since diagnosis, I have seen it. Some claim I mistook empathy for pity, but there's a thin line. Empathy understands while pity defines. I accepted empathy but fought pity because I didn't want its categorization. No one would cloak me in inability. My possibilities were up to me. My life was how I defined it because I am what I think. I am strong, loving, and beautiful, with all the attributes associated with positivity. Living in a world of love and self-affirmation is better than living in a universe of negativity.

Recipients of my weekly mile letters commented on my remarkable mental state. Through my words, they felt my spirit, upbeat and energetic. They called me an incredibly strong and blessed woman, and deemed me inspiring, amazing, and resilient. Their saying I was their inspiration humbled me.

While friends and family deemed me worthy of such accolades, I believed my tenacious attitude was what they noticed. To me, obstacles were pebbles and rocks, not boulders or mountains. Life's obstacles wanted me to sit on the curb, sulk, and wait for their removal, but why wait and brew frustration? I problem-solved or took a detour. Reaching the destination was the goal. Wasted time was wasted opportunity.

As the nurse drew my blood, I noticed a brochure on the bulletin board advertising a 5K to benefit the Adena Healing Garden, but the race was the day after my second round of chemo. Wait, why the hesitation? Wasn't this what I expected others not to do? The can't-do mentality was seeping into my thoughts. If I wanted to run, then there should be no second-guessing.

Entering mile 15, as I termed it to my friends and family in my last weekly letter, I felt great. I experienced no fatigue even after running five miles daily with Derek, all thirty pounds of him, in a jogging stroller while I tackled the challenging ascent of Yaples Orchard Drive. In addition, I ran seven miles on Saturday but could have run farther.

I asked for a race brochure. No copies were left, so the nurse who drew my blood went to make one. I grabbed the entry form from the nurse before leaving to have my first Neulasta shot, excited about the race and the project it would fund.

When I'd begun to think I could be Superwoman, the first side effect occurred. Outside some insomnia due to the steroid pills, I'd been unaffected by my first chemotherapy session. Then, Neulasta disrupted the streak. Though I took Claritin as directed, I woke up tired and achy; I felt like I had the flu, compounded by a whole-body bruise. Any touch, even a hug, caused discomfort, though not intolerable pain, so I told everyone I was not to be touched. My morning dragged on until an afternoon nap lessened the flu-like symptoms but not the bruising, which lingered for a few days. The flu-like symptoms were gone by the next day.

I continued to prepare for the Adena Healing Garden 5k. I supplemented my daily runs with Jillian Michaels' HIIT (high-intensity interval training) videos to increase my core strength. When they read about my upcoming race in the weekly letter, some family and friends donated to support the Healing Garden project. It touched me to know that they wanted to back this initiative. I knew I'd be unable to garner enjoyment from it, but I loved being part of a pay-it-forward moment.

On the morning of the race, I felt no ill effects from my five-hour chemotherapy session. Ready, I was striving for a personal best. The reasonably flat course was ideal, and the weather, a runner's dream, was cool and overcast. I proceeded to the pavilion and went to the preregistered lines to pick up my bib and shirt. Ken hung back with Derek and Aleya. While I waited in line, I saw an older woman in a pink 2013 Air Force Marathon in Training shirt. She was stretching on a bench on the other side of the pavilion. Inclined to converse with fellow marathoners, I walked toward her.

I introduced myself to Carol and inquired about the Air Force Marathon in Dayton, Ohio. Since Dayton was close, I was interested. I had heard the course was a single loop around the Air Force base for the half marathoners and a double loop for the marathoners. Spectators were minimal at specific points along the course. Having done Columbus, I was spoiled and used to excellent crowd support. Eventually, our conversation veered from running and marathon experiences to talking about ourselves. Carol discussed her grandkids' running and her husband's barbershop, which was near where I lived.

Carol was shocked to learn that I was racing despite being a cancer patient undergoing chemotherapy, and she was amazed at how healthy I looked. Impressed with my positive outlook and intention to compete in a fall marathon, she wished me luck as we proceeded to the starting area, where we parted but planned to meet after the race.

At the starting line, Ken took pictures. While he tried to persuade me to take off my sweatshirt, he failed. Typically, I raced in a T-shirt and shorts, but the air was chilly. Next, I put my ear pods into my ears. Due to the mastectomy, I had to hold my iPod rather than wear it in an armband, which made skipping songs much more effortless. Finally, I checked my Garmin and saw it was ready to clock my time. While I waited for the other runners and walkers to come to the starting line for our 9 AM start, I did some additional stretches to stay loose. Many cancer center workers, especially those who had just registered, commended my participation and were amazed by my determination and energy level.

Ken, Derek, and Aleya, proudly holding her dad's handmade sign, cheered as the gun went off. I followed the lead pack. I could tell that Carol was an excellent runner, so I tried to use her as my pacer. I kept her in view. I knew that beating her would be a tall order, but my goal was to stay as close to her as possible.

This being an out-and-back race, I could gauge my place performance. Near the mile-and-a-half turnaround, Carol was the lead female runner, while a mid-twenties woman, who had passed me earlier, was second. I was third, so I pushed my pace. Ultracompetitive, I wanted a medal.

About 400 meters from the finish line, I saw Aleya crouched behind Derek, who held Ken's handmade fluorescent-orange sign. It read RUN, MOMMY, RUN, with a smiley face in the upper right-hand corner. I heard Ken shout for me to run faster, so I assumed that another female runner was on my tail. I sprinted as fast as I could, and I heard Aleya scream, "Go, Mommy, go!" She raced alongside me for as long as she could, and continued to cheer me on to the finish line.

I stopped my Garmin as I crossed the finish line, knowing I hadn't beaten my best of 24:44, though my time, not far from it, was 25:03. I untied the sweatshirt I'd removed and tied around my waist mid-race and put it on, knowing I'd become cold. While I zipped my sweatshirt, Ken came and verified that I had medaled.

Amazed, Carol came and congratulated me. She couldn't believe how well I had run so soon after my second round of chemotherapy. As we continued to talk, others congratulated me, including the second-place woman's finisher, Amanda Steele. It turned out Ken worked with her at the paper mill.

At the medal ceremony, I was proud of what I had accomplished. Out of 105 runners, I placed third for the women. Ken took pictures while I walked up to receive my medal. When Ken asked for a group photo, Carol and Amanda agreed. Afterward, I told Carol I hoped to see her at a future race and wished her luck on her upcoming marathon.

As I walked back to the car, I glanced at my medal. I was happy with my ranking, but I'd wanted to run a personal best. Fortunately, I had future opportunities to accomplish that. Since signing up for the Adena Healing Garden 5K, I'd signed up—to Ken's dismay—for a few others. The Allen Elementary Running Club 5K, a week after my third chemo treatment, followed by Kill the Hill, a ten-mile race with two steep, seemingly never-ending hills eight days later. In addition, Cory, one of my fifth-grade colleagues, registered me for the Fire Run 5K a week after Kill the Hill and the day after my fourth round of chemo. When I jokingly asked if he was trying to kill me, he said I'd probably beat him to the finish line. Laughing, I replied that I probably would because I was that competitive.

While it may have seemed overwhelming, I felt confident. I had nothing to lose and everything to gain. Eventually, cancer would test my endurance, but until then, I would keep running.

Chapter Eighteen

The Fallen

Our greatest glory is not in never falling, but in rising every time we fall.

—Confucius

C oming off a few great weeks, I entered mile 17 with cancer letting me know I wasn't Superwoman. When I was ready to sleep on Monday night, cancer knocked down my cockiness. My second Neulasta shot obliterated me. Every joint in my body felt a level-10 pain. Too uncomfortable to sleep, I didn't know what to do. I couldn't ignore the throbbing that duplicated the beating of my heart. I felt bludgeoned, and wanted to lie in an ice bath to numb the pain, but instead, I left my bed in search of comfort I wouldn't find. I took ibuprofen, but it failed. I wanted to stay strong, but I could only cry and writhe in pain. The kids seemed befuddled.

Last week, I'd imagined my body telling the chemo drugs what the rules were. I imagined the white and red blood cells informing the chemo of my daily routine, my high-octane workouts, and how it shouldn't mess with me. I told Dr. Van-Deusen that I felt blessed to have had such a great week. I let the chemo know it wouldn't derail me, and my body kept it at bay. Unfortunately, Neulasta meted out a reality check.

In the morning, the sun rose, but I felt lifeless. To say I woke up would have meant I'd slept. I failed to get an ounce of sleep. Instead, I experienced a night of what felt like an extreme case of growing pains. Usually, Derek and I would play with his cars, train tracks, and puzzles or go outside and enjoy the weather, but the TV became the sitter. Fortunately, Derek didn't mind watching videos and playing with his cars if I was in the room. At that moment, I felt blessed. Derek accommodated my needs, whether he sensed them or not.

By Tuesday night, ibuprofen suppressed the pain from my hips to my lower extremities. Able to sleep, I wasn't bothered by the constant throbbing pain in my lower joints.

Wednesday, I awoke feeling slightly better. I drove Aleya to school and walked her to the front entrance. Once home, I changed into running clothes and put Derek in the jogging stroller. Still recuperating from my lack of sleep on Monday night, my body cried, *What are you thinking?* While I wanted to return to a daily running and workout routine, I didn't have the energy. During a two-mile run, I had to stop and walk. My engine failed to supply the power my body needed. Again, later that night, I took ibuprofen to relieve my lower-extremity joint pain. It was hard to be strong when I felt weak. I had set myself up for misunderstandings by being strong for my kids. When my energy was low, they didn't understand, and their expectations remained with me. Caring for my children, I tried to keep worry away, our daily routines on schedule, and the atmosphere happy. I wanted to project a strong mom, unaffected by cancer. The reality, however, was that even strong people become weak sometimes and need help. I hated to ask for help, so I upheld a hypocritical standard: though I told my students it was okay to ask for help, I didn't ask.

By Thursday, I bounced back. I no longer needed to rely on ibuprofen, and resumed playing with Derek, running my average of five miles, and doing my Jillian Michael DVD workouts. Having survived a second Neulasta shot, however, I didn't want a third.

After a painful and unproductive week, Mother's Day was an incredible upswing. Before my hourlong run, Derek greeted me with a bouquet three fourths his size. He was adorable. Who doesn't love a man who brings you flowers? Next, Trent and Aleya gave me homemade cards. According to Trent's, I was young and gorgeous. Yes, I was training him right! After my run, I took a shower, went to church with my family, and enjoyed a local Mother's Day brunch where the spread was marvelous. Then I took a well-deserved nap. To finish the day, we went bowling.

Thankfully, my bone pain preceded an important week full of events such as Trent's two track meets, Aleya's school musical, Trent's academic awards night, and Right to Read week, for which my fifth-grade colleagues, Brenda and Cory, asked me to read to our students. With my doctor's permission, I read them two stories. Excited to see me, they wanted to know when I would return. I told them not until next year, and they said they missed me.

I laughed and said, "Oh, *now* you miss me! What happened to 'You're working us too hard. You give us too much work! And you're so mean!' Now you appreciate me!" It was great to see my students, and being in my classroom gave me an energy rush.

Later that evening, Betsy, my neighbor, noticed my hand when our youngest boys were playing. When asked what happened, I said I didn't know. Four days following treatment, I started to scratch the itchy top of my right hand in the area where I'd had my second chemo treatment. I figured a mosquito had bitten me, but a few days later, I noticed a quarter-sized, oval-shaped red patch in that area. The skin was dry and scaly, and lotion provided only a temporary solution. It was slightly red in the morning and became redder as the day progressed.

When he arrived home from work, Betsy's husband, a dermatologist, examined it. He thought it looked like a fixed drug eruption and told me to look it up. I searched the term on my computer, and, after reading various medical articles and viewing the images that showed oval and red areas, I agreed with him. In addition, the articles mentioned Taxotere, one of my chemo medications. How might this affect my final two treatments?

After I'd put Derek to bed, I called Dr. VanDeusen about the fixed drug eruption. He suggested that a PICC might be best for the last two treatments. Then, I'd only have to worry about it for three weeks. Due to my skin reaction to the Taxotere, he didn't want to ruin my veins. Eventually, the redness would disappear, but he wanted me to send pictures of the area.

Having viewed the photos I'd taken earlier, he texted that it was neither an allergic reaction nor an eruption. The reaction resulted from the nurse's having put my injection through a smaller-bore vein in my hand. I was partially to blame, as I'd insisted she use the same arm after she'd blown the first vein, so she'd had to go lower. Consequently, my infusions needed to be slower, and the IV would need to be higher on my arm. Also, the last two would have to be administered into my right arm rather than the left. Eventually, the site of the injection reaction faded and disappeared.

Then, the doctor mentioned Mother's Day. As he's driven to church, he'd passed me running, and was amazed to see that I still had my hair. Jokingly, as if my hair could hear, I shushed him and said in a lighthearted tone, "Are you trying to jinx me?" In truth, I had lost some strands, but not enough to alarm me.

I walked downstairs and noticed that Ken was watching television. I sat on the couch across from his recliner. During the commercials, we discussed my conversation with

Dr. VanDeusen. I was confident the last two chemotherapy sessions would work out, but Ken's face showed that he was worried.

Then, I noticed more strands of hair on my clothing and around me on the couch. With each touch, three to four more fell. Had my luck been broken? Was this the I-told-you-so moment?

Ken commented that I saw my situation as the glass half full. He saw it as the glass half empty, and said I shouldn't be surprised by hard times with chemotherapy. This week was a struggle, but I was unwilling to fall to cancer. Had I fallen victim to a superhero complex? Or did it keep me strong rather than vulnerable?

The next morning, I answered the phone. It was my gynecologist's office, or so I thought. The receptionist said I was overdue for my regular checkup. I mentioned that I hadn't called to schedule my annual appointment because I was in the middle of chemotherapy treatments, and a Pap smear would be inaccurate due to the presence of TC in my body. As I finished, I doubled back. Wait—did she say Dr. Victor's office? The receptionist's silence made me realize that I had admitted my current situation to another person several states away in an office where I was no longer a patient. I apologized for mistaking her for my current gynecologist's staffer, and asked if Dr. Victor had forwarded the records I'd requested last year. She checked. They had sent the documents, but my patient file didn't indicate my move or a new gynecologist. Before we ended the call, she asked more questions, and like many others, was shocked by my diagnosis.

I hung up the phone, and thought Dr. Victor and Dr. Beffler were guardian angels. Without Dr. Victor's suggestion of an early mammogram, I wouldn't have had the preliminary testing that had sent me to Dr. Beffler due to my dense breast tissue. Had I not followed Dr. Beffler's follow-up advice, I could have found my cancer later, which would have given it more time to progress.

Chapter Nineteen

Hair Today, Gone Tomorrow

Every experience, no matter how bad it seems, holds within it a blessing of some kind. The goal is to find it.

—Buddha

DON'T TOUCH. Museums place this sign near valuable artwork. I wanted to put it on my head as single strands fell randomly, but nothing would've helped. My luck had run out, and the chemo was making its presence known. When I sat, I felt fallen hairs tickle my shoulder or the back of my neck. When I washed dishes, I saw them afloat in the water. They accumulated on my pillow and sheets. Finally, when I was inclined to touch my hair, I held strands in the palm of my hand. Expected results should have met with less shock.

I ran a quick three miles on the Friday following Mother's Day. Afterward, I debated whether to wash my hair. It had been a few days. I was afraid, but refusing to wash my hair would only prolong an unwanted outcome. I needed to accept the inevitable, whether today, tomorrow, or next week. I grabbed the shampoo bottle, closed the shower door, and hoped for the best.

I swiped my fingers gently through my hair, and looked down as the lather washed away. No strands clogged the drain or littered the shower floor. I turned off the water, wrung my hair, grabbed a towel, and patted it dry. On the towel, I saw strands.

I knew that it wasn't good to brush tangled, wet hair, but I did it anyway. Swipe after swipe, my hairbrush collected more of my long dark-brown strands. Finally, after I'd cleaned the brush several times and seen half my trashcan filled with wads of hair, I stopped. Done, I grabbed my knotted, tangled hair and pulled it into a ponytail.

Turning my head from side to side, I looked at my matted hair. Touching my ponytail, I pulled away more loose hairs. Tears formed. My long, dark, thick, beautiful hair—once a reason why John Casablancas's modeling agency had chosen me to spokesmodel for Pantene at a retail store in the Philadelphia area—was leaving me. I covered my hair with my hands and imagined myself bald. Could I do this? Could I shave the tresses I loved to style and run my hands through? *Yes*, I thought, but my mind cried a quick *no*.

Throughout the day, the shedding continued. I felt like a dog, and I was tired, tired of individual strands falling out and tired of traipsing to the garbage can. Cancer had control, but not for much longer. I picked up the phone and dialed my salon. Unfortunately, Jen, my stylist, was unavailable, so I made an appointment with one of her coworkers.

One of my colleagues, a former Marine, offered to perform the shaving Semper Fi style, Ken and I decided a salon would be best for Derek. Admittedly, I was keen on having a former Marine shave my head, since it would have been very me and somewhat symbolic. *The few, the proud, the breast-cancer warrior* had a nice ring to it.

The next day, I left my older children at home with my husband, put Derek in his car seat, and headed to CVS. Without hair to accent my face, I felt a need for makeup. I rarely wore any, so I had no eyeliner, eye shadow, or blush at home, and my lipstick was nearly a year old. It felt weird to walk down the makeup aisle; a complete 360. My grandmother had ingrained the importance of embracing natural beauty when I was young, and it had stuck. I'd hated wearing makeup for modeling school, photo shoots, and jobs. The mask-like feel of foundation and powder made me want to wash my face. For my wedding, I wanted to wear none, but Mom insisted, so we compromised. I wore eyeliner, eye shadow, blush, and lipstick. Now I was in a makeup aisle buying cosmetics I rarely used. I left with my purchases, and headed to A Cut Above, feeling like a traitor to my inner self.

As I carried Derek into the salon, I saw a gentleman and two stylists. Roseanne, in a pink-and-white-striped shirt and a pink scarf, directed me to her chair. I wondered if she'd worn the colors on purpose. I didn't have the heart to tell her, figuring her motive was empathetic, how much I hated pink. Seated in the chair, I put Derek on my lap so he faced the mirror. Roseanne put the cape around my neck and showed me the clip she wanted to use to shave my head. She mentioned her friend's participation in the Susan G. Komen Race for the Cure in Columbus that morning, which showed her connection to the cause. Roseanne reminisced about her friend's initial hair loss during a boat ride. As the wind whipped through the friend's hair, it blew strands away. Not knowing how to respond, I listened quietly.

As she prepared her station, Roseanne mentioned how empowered I must have felt. When I called the salon, I had felt empowered. Now, seated in the chair, I felt relieved and anxious. No more trips to the garbage can; no more worry about waking up bald; no more stress about when to shave my head. Still, the unknown was troubling. What would I look like, and would Derek accept my new look? He was my distraction as much as my focus. My reaction would influence his, so I remained steadfast and lighthearted. Amazingly, I was in good spirits.

Roseanne cut off my ponytail and handed it to me. I put it in a sandwich bag. Next, Rosanne laid the scissors down and prepped the shaver with the proper clip to give me a sporty crewcut.

In the mirror, I saw Derek's confusion. His stare verified that I'd made the right decision. How does one explain this to a two-year-old? As my hair fell, I looked at him, smiled, and said, "Mommy is getting her hair cut."

I asked if he wanted to feel my head, and guided his hand without waiting for an answer. Derek grimaced in horror, and he pulled his hand away from mine. I stopped. His eyes locked on my face. Spooked, he felt uncomfortable. I prayed the moment would pass without him crying. I smiled, and talked about my haircut in a positive tone. I never once looked down; I just lifted and dropped what hair landed on him to the floor.

Rosanne finished. She put the clippers down and removed the cape, then handed me a mirror. She and the other stylist commented on my perfectly shaped head and how I had a diamond-shaped area where my soft spot, the fontanelle, would have been when I was a baby. Rosanne gave my chair a half turn as I held the mirror in front of my face. She pointed out three bald patches, each no bigger than a dime. Based on how much hair I'd lost, I was amazed at their small size.

Roseanne then led me to a chair and wrapped a towel around my neck. I leaned back and nestled my neck into the headrest of the basin. Roseanne pumped a few squirts of shampoo into one hand, and turned the water on with the other. Having less hair affected my sensation; the water that sprayed my scalp was freezing. Roseanne noticed my flinch, and she turned the faucet to WARM. Feeling the warmth, I relaxed. While Roseanne shampooed my head, she pointed out that my scalp had a few dry patches, a side effect of chemotherapy, and recommended using a conditioner to moisturize my scalp.

I prepared to leave after she rubbed my head dry. Roseanne mentioned how beautiful I looked, which stroked my ego. I felt as beautiful as her compliment suggested. My grandmother, Violet, always said I had a pretty face. Fortunately, ancestral genes had blessed me with one. Without hair on my head, my face was more pronounced.

When I asked Roseanne how much I owed, she said, "Nothing." I insisted she accept a tip. Reluctantly, she took it, thanked me, and wished me well. I picked up Derek, opened the door, and walked to the car. As we drove, I pondered my family's reactions.

Once home, I revealed my buzz cut. Ken said I looked better than Sinead O'Connor and lovingly offered to shave his head in support. With a wink and a smile, I told him to appreciate his hair while he still had it. My daughter's sad expression showed that she missed my long, dark hair. I knelt so I was at eye level, and held her hands as I assured her my hair would grow back. Ken concurred. My teenage son walked through the kitchen, smiled at me, and said I still looked gorgeous.

That evening was my first public reveal. I needed to buy a baptismal and a graduation card. Halfway down the hill, I noticed I'd forgotten my hat and decided not to return home for it. While I knew others might look at me, I was ready. I entered Walgreens, headed for the card aisle, and chose my cards. On the way to pay, I passed a child, her look questioning. Depending on one's viewpoint, she was neither bold nor impolite. Kids try to make sense of the world, but social etiquette hinders their curiosity. I would have answered her questions with no hard feelings. Perhaps it was the teacher in me.

Still confident in my baldness, I offered to go to Central Hardware for lawn bags the next day, but this time I remembered my hat. In the lawn and garden section, I scanned the shelves. A saleswoman approached and offered her help. Without it, I would never have found them. She guided me to the back of the store, showed me the trash-bag aisle, and pointed to the bottom shelf. I thanked her, grabbed a pack of brown lawn bags, and headed to checkout. Once there, the saleswoman offered to take me to another counter, but she had an ulterior motive. When she asked if I'd cut my hair for the summer, I told her, though I figured she knew, that I had breast cancer.

She moved her fingers through her curly, silver-gray hair with pride, and said that she'd had breast cancer too. We swapped stories. While I had a mammogram as preventative screening, she requested one due to health concerns. I'd heard the words "serious concerns," while she'd heard that she was okay, but her doctors were wrong, and she was right. We discussed various topics such as stages, numbers, support groups, reconstruction, and our husbands' responsibilities and supportiveness. Although our experiences were different, our attitudes toward cancer were the same. Her husband utilized FMLA to assist and take her to chemotherapy, while Ken used vacation time and worked from home. I had decided to do reconstruction while she didn't.

Paying for my purchase, I saw her write, "T2 N0 M0. I am glad I got that off my chest," on a small piece of paper. She handed it to me and explained that a girlfriend had made her a shirt with this message. T2 meant a single tumor with a diameter between 2.1 to 5 cm, N0 meant the lymph nodes were clean, and M0 meant clean margins or no cancer outside the breast tumor. Her girlfriend's message was correct. The cost of one's chest was worth one's life.

As another customer approached, the two saleswomen stated how good I looked in my white Nike Dri-Fit baseball cap. Opinions differed on why. While the older one credited my bone structure and complexion, the younger saleswoman credited my eyes. I credited my smile.

I grabbed the lawn bags and walked away from the register. Before I left, the older woman advised me to use masking tape or a lint roller if my crewcut became patchy, and told me to experience standing in the rain, as the feeling was gratifying. I found it odd that I'd met another cancer survivor so soon. Coincidence? No. Through a breast-cancer survivor and others, God was working. He told me I was beautiful, hair or no hair. Besides, to stand bald in the rain would be an experience worth having.

As I bagged Derek's dirty diaper the following morning, he reached for my hat, removed it, swiped his hand along my head, then put my hat back. His happy expression relieved me. No longer scared, he had embraced my stubble. Derek's action affirmed my decision. Bringing him to the salon had given him peace and confirmed that Mommy was still Mommy and not an alien.

To either sex, hair is the ultimate accessory to style. Initially, I felt a tinge of sadness and hesitation over my loss. My hair, just like my breasts, was a casualty; however, my attitude became carefree and confident. My hair would grow back, but my life would not. If actresses could lose their locks to play a role and feel beautiful, so could I. Frankly, my inner tomboy relished the simplicity.

Chapter Twenty

A Square Peg in a Round Hole

Anxiety weighs down the human heart, but a good word cheers it up.

—Proverbs 12:25 (NRSV)

With my hair gone, it was evident that something was awry. Eyes questioned what they saw. I wanted conversation to revolve around the daily monotonies of life, not cancer, so I used people's cautiousness to my advantage. They fished for an answer, but I didn't bite. When asked how I was, I replied, "Fine." I knew they wanted to know, but I wouldn't confirm or deny it. Would it hurt others whom I chose not to inform of my cancer? Perhaps. Nonetheless, I decided to be selfish, accept the consequences, offer no explanations, and ask for forgiveness later.

Five days after my haircut, I attended an afternoon Look Good Feel Good session sponsored by the American Cancer Society at the Adena Cancer Center. I wanted to learn how to wear scarves. Though eligible for a free wig from the Komen Foundation, I preferred hats, especially my Nike Featherlight Dri-Fit caps, but I wanted to wear scarves to church and on special occasions.

I entered the conference room fifteen minutes late. Ten women watching an introductory video about the Look Good Feel Good workshop experience sat behind tables arranged in a U formation. Directed to sign in, I wrote my name, address, and type of cancer. Breast cancer was the minority. Near the front of the screen, a woman wiped tears from her eyes. I felt too chipper and out of place, so I sat near the snack table, away from the other participants.

After the video, a volunteer pointed me toward the only vacant chair available among the women as another volunteer handed me a dark fuchsia cosmetic bag labeled FAIR. When the volunteers began with skincare and makeup, I sighed. With a tight window before I had to pick up Aleya, I wished scarves and hair care had been first. Though I rarely used makeup, I'd learned how to apply it during my modeling school days.

Eventually, I spoke to the woman on my right, who had lung cancer. I was surprised to not detect a raspy voice or smoker's cough, and asked her how she'd discovered her cancer. She had injured her shoulder playing with her grandkids. When the injury didn't improve, she'd had an x-ray. It showed her shoulder injury as well as lung cancer. While her husband smoked only outside the house, she'd never smoked. Like me, she was an anomaly. How does one get lung cancer when one has never smoked? Secondhand smoke may have been the cause, but it seemed so cruel.

After hearing her story, I shared mine. She expressed interest, not sympathy, and our talk helped dissipate my feelings of awkwardness. It was a casual conversation without tears or anger. Our surprising diagnoses helped us relate, and we shared a common goal. When I told her about Mary Bryant, the woman who'd inspired me to run my fall marathon, a staff member overheard and interjected that Mary was an exception and that her story was marginal.

There it was—confirmation that my perspective didn't fit. I was flying solo. My mind fumed; my mouth was silent. Everyone can be an exception. Let me rephrase: *Everyone is exceptional.* Cancer is a negative, but it doesn't have to cancel one's optimism or ability to dream, to be strong, and to think big. In this room, every woman could set her own goal. The marathon was my goal, but one could strive for a shorter mileage, a certain number of minutes, or a different type of exercise. Why did cancer convey a shroud of incapacity?

My exercise regimen and positive attitude contributed to the minimal side effects of chemotherapy. Why not encourage others? Hadn't Dr. VanDeusen assured me exercise was beneficial? When I asked if I could exercise too much, he said no, then cited a study in which genetically altered mice that had been injected with breast-cancer tumors ran in their wheels for six miles a day showed a reduction in tumor size and growth. Based on these results, researchers had patients run on treadmills for forty-five minutes following chemo treatments. In addition, having reviewed studies on exercise training and cancer survivorship, an American College of Sports Medicine panel in July 2010 concluded that exercise training was "safe during and after cancer treatments and results in improvements in physical functioning, quality of life, and cancer-related fatigue." If exercise minimized patients' side effects and decreased their chances of reoccurrence, why not recommend and promote it?

I watched the clock and decided to leave. I told the woman I would keep her in my prayers, and exited the Look Good Feel Better session feeling like the black sheep. Negativity loves to combat positivity. In that room, I was too optimistic for some, but I wouldn't let the staff member's comments deter me. Everyone's reaction to bad news and challenging situations was different. For me, it was important to rise from the rubble. Running was my rising moment.

In addition, the staff member's words solidified why I'd chosen not to go to any support-group meetings. I had received monthly group notices, but refused to go. Like today, optimism wouldn't be in attendance. I didn't want negative words or actions to snuff mine. My mindset was my lifeline. No one had permission to take an ax through my words or actions and chip away at what I'd built.

Was I being selfish? Was I meant to inspire? Could I change other patients' mindsets, or would I step on their toes? I reflected on the younger woman across from me, who seemed attentive to what I'd been saying to my neighbor. Then the receptionist asked me how I liked the program.

I told her about having missed the part I wanted to hear, and I saw Dr. VanDeusen approach the corner. This was the first time he'd seen me since I'd had my head shaved, and he joked that our last phone conversation had made him wonder whether he'd given me the correct dosage, especially after seeing me with a full head of hair on Mother's Day. In jest, I said, "You jinxed me." Then I laughingly told him he hadn't jinxed me, but I found the timing ironic. My hair had lasted five weeks and a day, which had made my oncologist second-guess himself.

In the following weeks, my hair ceased to fall, which made me question whether I'd shaved my head too soon. Then I noticed more stubble on my pillow. My hair was thinning, but it was growing back in some areas, an unexplainable phenomenon. I'd seen videos and read blogs that documented hair growth, which usually begins to regrow a month or two after chemotherapy. Pleased to see new growth, I decided to appreciate the prospect, knowing that the third treatment could bring it to an end.

Chapter Twenty-One

Sisterhood

*Sweet is the voice of a sister in the season of sorrow,
and wise is the counsel of those who love us.*

—Benjamin Disraeli

My ball caps and the stubble on my head became calling cards. Suddenly, women I'd never met began to approach me everywhere. After introductions, I understood. Our commonality was cancer. Concerned, these women shared their ordeals, supportive words of encouragement, advice, prayers, and love. We discussed challenges and celebrated victories. To verify that cancer's effects would pass, they showed me their hair growth and sometimes even their mastectomy scars. Strangers became sisters willing to pray for me and let me know I was going to be okay.

In January, the month of my diagnosis, I'd wanted no part of this sisterhood. Membership meant having cancer. Their insignia was the pink ribbon. While some proudly wore pink, the quintessential female color, I abhorred it as much as I did cancer.

Before breast cancer, I would never have seen myself as part of a sisterhood. Now, I'm a member of one of the largest in the U.S.—breast-cancer survivors. Our chapters were numerous, from local to worldwide, but there was no selection process or bid day. The only eligibility requirement was cancer. Invaded, not recruited, I hated being eligible. Cancer didn't care. Initiated on my diagnosis day, I wasn't even a legacy. I wasn't the daughter, sister, or granddaughter of a member. I was the first. I gained a sisterhood not by choice but by an unknown circumstance, and I hoped to be the last in my bloodline.

My Big was AnnMarie Vinges, a colleague at my former school district. AnnMarie's diagnosis came three years before I left the Scotch-Plains-Fanwood district. To know that she'd battled breast cancer while a wife and the mother of two young girls made me feel she'd be a tremendous asset in answering patients' questions. At first, I felt awkward; I thought that perhaps she would rather live and forget, but I had underestimated the love, faith, and commitment this sisterhood held for its members. The sisterhood was more than willing to help. Sisters of cancer were there for each other anytime and anywhere. While our stories and conditions were unique, our similarities were there. As a patient, however, you need more than a computer and a competent team of doctors.

Thankfully, AnnMarie helped me make this discovery. Her guidance was invaluable, and her commitment limitless. She was my mentor, cheerleader, confidante, and friend. With the words "I do not regret my mastectomy" and "Please don't worry, you are going to be fine," she was my rock. If she could conquer stage-2 breast cancer, I could conquer stage 1. She and my sisters, known and unknown, were evidence that women were more resilient than cancer.

So competitive, aren't we, my sisters and me? Damn right we are!

Chapter Twenty-Two

Armor of Humor

Always laugh when you can, it is cheap medicine.

—Lord Byron

I love to laugh. It's essential to find humor in life. I'm no comedian, but I love to be funny. My attempts at humor usually take the form of wordplay: I change or use the lyrics of a song to fit the moment or use something situational. My humor isn't sarcastic, dark, or raunchy. Instead, I love to let myself be just plain silly from time to time. Humor is a necessary diversion in life.

Before my surgery, I joked about my breasts, jested about turning in my old saggy, breastfed, stretch-marked breasts for a new set. As for size, my male colleagues, Bob and Cory, were willing to help me create the set list that ranged from how and why Ken should have a say in my size to giving myself black eyes or causing car accidents while running. Others might have found this topic vulgar or thought I'd crossed a line, but I was as much a participant as the audience for this improvisational act. Having breast cancer was so absurd that I had to laugh. Laughter combatted sorrow.

While my attitude shouted denial to some, there was no denying I had cancer, but I handled it my way. Positivity and lightheartedness were my daily vitamins for a healthy mind-set, and my positive attitude may have prevented some of the chemotherapy's side effects.

During my third treatment, Ken and I started a discussion that led me to burst into hearty laughter. While not meant to be a condemnation, his comment, merely an observation that I was laughing in the chemo wing, made me feel guilty.

That moment made me recall my grandfather's viewing. Like a funeral parlor, there were some places where laughter was deemed inappropriate and was ill-received. Nonetheless, as my cousins and I reminisced about our grandfather, the man we loved dearly, we began to laugh. As our laughter permeated the silence, my grandmother scolded us. She missed his presence, as did we, and she asked us to show respect. Happy memories, however, a gift of comfort, relieved our sorrow, if only for a moment.

Yes, I was in the chemotherapy wing, surrounded by patients consumed by their emotions. Yet, while some may have been sad or dealing with cancer's destructive mindset, I refused to feel guilt or be intimidated by cancer. Every time it tried to drag me into its quicksand of negativity, I wouldn't take the bait. I knew God wouldn't want me to. Romans 12:2 (NRSV) states, "Do not be conformed to this world, but be transformed by the renewing of your minds, so that you may discern what is the will of God—what is good and acceptable and perfect." Though serious, cancer wouldn't make me conform or strip me of my laughter.

From the third chemotherapy session to the last, I was running home. With three consecutive weekends of racing, the third the day after my final chemo, I looked forward to accomplishing some personal bests. Fortunately, I continued to experience no side effects, and felt unwavering strength and tireless endurance.

The first of my three races, the Allen Elementary 5K, a final showcase for the Allen Elementary Running Club, had more children than adult runners. The course began and ended at the Chillicothe High School parking lot, with a slight hill toward the finish line. Having taken an interest in joining her school's running club, Aleya decided to run rather than cheerlead for this one, which made it the first race we ever ran together.

Though the temperature was slightly warmer than during the last race, it was still idyllic. Throughout the course, I pushed for a personal best. Unfortunately, despite giving it my all, I fell short of at 25:10. This was slower than my previous race, but I knew I couldn't compare the times because the courses were different. After finishing, I turned around, found Aleya, and ran with her for 600m until I stopped to cheer and watch as she crossed the finish line.

A week later, I ran Kill the Hill, a ten-mile race that supported the operation of the Adena Mansion, the 2,000-acre estate of Thomas Worthington (1773–1827), sixth governor of Ohio and one of the state's first U.S. Senators. Again, the morning greeted me with beautiful running weather, and I felt alert and energetic. On the way to the race, Ken asked if I wanted to back down to the 5K.

I thought back to 2007, my first ten-mile race experience, laughed, and said, "This isn't my first rodeo!" In 2007, however, I'd found it a challenge. I came home and lay down on the living room floor, too tired and sore to do anything. Having trained for a marathon, I'd come far, but compared to 26.2, a ten-miler was easy.

I checked in, gave Ken my registration goodie bag, pinned my number to my black Clima-lite Adidas running shirt, and strapped my hydration bag around my waist. Then I adjusted my white Nike Dri-Fit hat, put my iPod earbuds in my ears, and walked toward the start.

When the gun went off, I pressed my Garmin to clock my time once I crossed the start line. I passed the lookout on my way to descend what I would eventually ascend at the start of mile 9. The lookout enabled me to see across the Scioto River Valley to the Logan Range, the inspiration for the Great Seal of the State of Ohio. After descending Adena Hill, I ran on a gravel path until I began the ascent up Yaples Orchard Drive, the first of the two long hills. While the 5K runners turned around, I pushed up the long, winding hill. Once I reached the top, I knew the rest of the run would be easy until I started mile 9.

I made sure to hydrate, especially on the floodwall where there was little to no shade, and I felt great. Some spectators were cheering runners throughout the course, but most would be waiting at the finish line. As I crossed over from the path to the street that led to Adena, I knew I was on pace to break my previous record. All I had to do was run up Adena Hill without stopping. Putting one foot in front of the other, I started strong but reached a point where I felt I was climbing rather than running as the slope increased. I felt relief when I'd nearly crested the hill, knowing the finish was less than half a mile away. I heard the spectators and pushed harder to reach the flatter part of the finish. As I rounded the bend, I saw the inflatable finish arch, and sprinted with everything left in the tank.

As I crossed the finish line, I stopped my Garmin and looked at my time, 1:35:17. I'd run a personal best, taking six minutes off the previous year's run. I smiled and did a Montell Jordan "This is How We Do It" celebratory dance move. To think Ken had wanted me to drop down to the 5K—shame on him!

Coming off a runner's high, I entered another, even bigger, high on June 12, 2013, my last chemotherapy session. As the nurses congratulated me, they told me that although they wanted to see me go, they hated to see me go. I was their star patient. In twenty-one days I would be chemo free. Except for my hair loss, the Neulasta joint and bone pain, and the injection reaction, I had managed to avoid many of the side effects, and I hoped to finish the same way.

The following morning was my last scheduled 5K, the Fire Run, which supported a local volunteer fire department. When my teaching colleague, Cory, had told me nearly a month prior that he had registered me to run, I didn't know if I'd have the energy. Now, I was ready to beat him. Many of my Mt. Logan colleagues were also there to run or walk. They commented on how great I looked and how inspiring it was to see me run through chemotherapy. In addition, I saw other runners there whom I'd competed with in previous races.

I walked to the line, ready for another personal best. As the gun went off, I started fast and didn't look back. Like the Allen 5K, it took place in Yoctangee Park. As I wound through the park, I kept a steady pace and eyed Cory's position. We neared the finish line, and I knew he wasn't far behind, but I still had a lead. Wanting to win, I kicked it into another gear and ran to the finish with all I had left. I checked my Garmin and saw I had shaved thirty seconds off my 5K personal best!

I made my way over to Ken, who was with two other runners I'd seen at Kill the Hill. He introduced me to Deb and Pam. They wanted me to join their local running club. In addition, they mentioned a sixteen-mile trail race on Saturday. I looked at Ken and could tell he was worried. He knew me well. While I wanted to say yes, my conscience said, *Probably not a good idea*, as I wasn't the best trail runner. Because I always wanted to run fast, I'd tripped over rocks or tree roots and had often hurt myself on trail runs, so I declined, but I decided to join them for morning runs. With marathon training underway, having other runners to run with would be great.

As Ken, the kids, and I were leaving, Cory approached with a smile and said, "I can't believe the woman with cancer beat me."

Laughing, I said, "She sure did! Let me know if you ever want a rematch."

Chapter Twenty-Three

Survivor?

One who believes in himself has no need to convince others.

—Laozi

At the end of June, Ken, the kids, and I attended a cancer survivor's picnic sponsored by the Adena Cancer Center at the V.A. Memorial Stadium, where the Chillicothe Paints, a collegiate wooden bat baseball team in the Prospect League, played. When the invitation arrived at the end of May, I called to reserve five tickets.

Closer to the event, I began to ponder the term "survivor." When did survivorship officially begin? Was it the day of my last chemo treatment, twenty-one days after that, or the day of my mastectomy?

Was I cancer free? I didn't know. I assumed I was once Dr. Sickle-Santanello cut it out of me back on March 1, but I'd needed chemotherapy to ensure less risk of recurrence. I'd felt chemotherapy was the extended life-insurance policy worth my peace of mind. Every cell needed cleansing of cancer's destructive ability.

In search of answers, I talked with Ken, a few members of the local running club I had joined, and my dad. I wanted to make sure I'd made the right decision. I asked the question, and each of them had a different response.

Like me, Ken struggled over whether cancer survivors would define me as a survivor. What defines a survivor? In his eyes, I was a fighter; therefore I was a survivor. He told me to go.

During a long run early Saturday morning, I posed the question to my running group. Instantaneously, Pam shot me an incredulous look as if to say, "Are you kidding me?" Then, in true Pam fashion, she said, "You're not dead, right?"

I chuckled. Pam's response ended the conversation. To her, I wasn't dead; therefore I was a survivor.

My dad's answer was immediate: "When you think you are one."

He reminded me of a high school indoor track invitational during my sophomore year. I was running an 800m heat with four other runners. When permitted to leave our assigned lanes, we moved as a tight pack into lane one, vying for the lead. Suddenly, my feet tangled with another competitor's, and I fell to the track and first place disappeared. Crying, I heard Dad yell, "Get up!"

Those words snapped me out of my pity party. I smacked the track and sprinted the remaining 300 meters to finish. My coach, who was astonished by my second-place finish, saw how anger had given me the adrenaline to do the impossible, and he sought to recreate my rage at every meet. For the rest of the track season, the ongoing joke was to get me angry before a race.

Life was like this moment. First, unforeseen complications could make you fall, but you had a choice—quit or get up. Dad reminded me that to finish proclaimed my strength.

Upon arrival, the volunteers asked us to sign in and gave me a survivor bag. Inside was an insulated cold-drink cup with the word "Survivor" written in purple. In addition, we received tickets for food and drinks. Fortunately, a canopy shaded the food and picnic tables because the evening was hot and humid. We found a picnic table to stash our belongings, and headed to the food tent.

As we stood in line to get our food, the traditional summer ballgame fare, I observed the crowd around me. I was the youngest cancer survivor there. It shouldn't have surprised me, but it did. The survivors, all elderly, were there with their husbands and grown adult children. My kids were the youngest.

I grabbed a plate, napkin, and a set of utensils, and decided between hamburgers and hotdogs, potato and macaroni salad, various chip bags, and dessert choices of fruit, sheet cake, and assorted cookies. I had to harness Derek's desire to grab multiple desserts. As we passed through the line, I greeted Dr. VanDeusen and nurses from the cancer center who served the food and helped run the event.

I took Derek's and my food back to the picnic table and looked over the baseball field. Derek wanted to run toward the wooden railing that separated our area from the left field, and I followed him. Unable to see over it, he tried to look through the slates. Then he stretched out his arms and looked at me. I held him, and remained there for the national anthem and the first pitch, thrown by an elderly prostate cancer survivor. Finally, we returned to the table.

Later, an elderly woman approached me when I was disposing of my trash. She noted my hair growth, and asked how long it had been since my last chemo. She looked surprised to hear "Last Friday," but I expected that reaction. From YouTube videos and blogs about hair growth, I'd learned it could take two to three months after treatments. Already having stubble, however, I was grateful.

When we left the picnic area, Ken, the kids, and I walked past the third-base line; we wanted to sit behind home plate. In the stands, survivors sat with their families. Some wore group T-shirts that honored their journey, or ribbon shirts that denoted the type of cancer they'd had. Being surrounded by survivors made me think of survivorship.

The picnic's purpose was to honor cancer survivors. When I received the invite, I thought that meant being free of the disease. Having beaten cancer, we lived. I was right, but I was wrong too. By definition, a survivor is a person who remains alive or copes well with life's difficulties. If that meant beating death, no one is a survivor. Survivors like my Aunt Rose, who didn't allow cancer to take away from being a mom and wife, hadn't lived but had fought hard.

In the end, cancer takes no one. God does. He begins our mission on Earth and He decides when it's complete. Cancer may cause our bodies to fail, but it doesn't take our souls. Cancer is a medical explanation that allows the coroner to provide a reason for death. Our body, a vessel, is not who we are. Our spirit defines us. Our corpse doesn't contain our personality, viewpoints, quirks, love, spirituality, intellect, motivations, or desires. We are all survivors making our way and our mark along the path called life until our Heavenly Father calls us to return home.

Chapter Twenty-Four

Presumptions and Actuality

Thoughts become perception, perception becomes reality.
Alter your thoughts, alter your reality.

—William James

As a young kid, I was a late bloomer due to my active lifestyle as a gymnast and a runner. In fifth grade, my girlfriends were buying their first training bras and maxi pads while I was still wearing T-shirts and waiting. Shopping for my first training bra was premature, but I wanted to be part of the conversation. By college, I filled out to a 36-C. I thought my breasts were proportional to my five-foot-six, 130-pound frame, though some friends and family thought I was well endowed and wished for what I had.

I joked about turning in my old breasts for a new pair of manufactured silicone ones; they couldn't recreate the exact look or sensation, but I thought they'd come close. I would have scars and possible wrinkling and dimpling with reconstruction, but looked forward to perkier breasts with no stretch marks. I failed, however, to realize reconstruction's limitations.

Though recent studies refuted the initial claims that silicone causes cancer, I felt uneasy choosing silicone implants, but

I wanted breasts. I wanted to be back to my original size. The problem was that implants came in cc's, not cup sizes. Therefore it was hard to determine when to stop the fills. Due to the fill Dr. Holland had performed during my mastectomy, I had mini-bumps. I felt minimal discomfort with each additional fill until the last. It hurt when I ran. Based on how it felt and what I saw, I thought I had reached a size to my liking, but my husband disagreed. He thought I needed a few more fills to attain what I'd once had.

With chemotherapy completed, I wanted to schedule reconstructive surgery as soon as possible, but Ken preferred I wait at least a month. He wanted my body to recuperate from chemo, and give my white and red blood cells and platelets time to increase. Dr. VanDeusen agreed. As long as I could start the school year with my new class, I was okay with waiting a month. After Friday's oncologist visit, I would meet with Dr. Holland and learn the surgery date and time.

As for my arm, I thought I'd have had complete mobility by then, but I was still doing daily exercises. I had full movement of my left arm, but could only extend my right arm slightly above my ear before I felt pain. When I lifted my right arm to the point of discomfort, I felt a rope-like sensation from armpit to elbow. To try to make sense of this, I searched the internet. I typed "arm movement after mastectomy—rope-like feel from armpit to elbow," and saw many results for axillary web syndrome (AWS) or cording.

I read multiple articles about AWS, and was sure this was what I had. The description and circumstances around why it formed matched my situation. First, I could feel a web of thick, rope-like structures under my arm. Second, it commonly occurs with surgical breast cancer procedures such as mastectomy, lumpectomy, sentinel-node biopsy, or axillary lymph-node dissection. Out of the four, I'd had two. The articles mentioned some suggested exercises as well as physical therapy. Having heard Anne Marie discuss her painful physical therapy process to regain arm movement, I hoped PT would be unnecessary. I knew I'd find out more tomorrow, so I pushed the thought aside.

As I walked into Dr. Sickle-Santanello's office, I reminisced about my first visit when I'd seen a woman leave with the familiar black-and-pink bag. I prayed she would find the strength needed to read the book. I signed in at the registration counter, then sat and watched the turtle Derek had marveled at in late January. I hadn't been in the office since late March when the doctor had permitted me to hold Derek. Back then, I'd mentioned the soreness in my right arm, but Dr. Sickle-Santanello believed that holding more weight, such as carrying Derek, would strengthen the tendons and help them heal faster. Unfortunately, it hadn't. I heard my name called, and I went into the room to wait.

Dr. Sickle Santanello opened the door and said, "Well, if it isn't the star patient!"

Laughing, I said, "Yes, I guess I am an overachiever."

She shut the door, sat down on her stool, and proceeded to discuss the next step, hormone therapy. Since my breast cancer tumors were hormone-receptor positive, Tamoxifen, a pill that blocks estrogen and progesterone, was recommended. Due to my young age, the doctor suggested I take Tamoxifen for ten years rather than five, which would further reduce my risk of recurrence. I wouldn't begin to take the daily medication until two weeks after my reconstructive surgery, since Tamoxifen had a 1 percent chance of causing blood clots. I appreciated her erring on the side of caution.

Next, I asked about my right arm. I explained that it felt painful when I tried to straighten my arm above my head, and that if I raised my arm, I could see a tendon protruding from my armpit. She suggested physical therapy. I wasn't thrilled, but I'd need physical therapy if I didn't want it to worsen. Thinking the surgery could aggravate the tendon more, I decided to wait to start PT until after reconstruction. We decided to discuss physical therapy in September, when I would see the doctor again to discuss my follow-up bloodwork.

I left Dr. Sickle-Santanello's office and I drove to Mt. Carmel Hospital, where Dr. Holland told me that my final outpatient reconstruction surgery would be done on Friday, July 26. Afterward, I would have drains for a week and couldn't lift for four weeks. I'd need help arranging my classroom, but the end was in view.

A few weeks before reconstruction surgery, I faltered. I wondered if I'd made a mistake by stopping the fills, and questioned whether I would be the same size as before my mastectomy. Like a movie trailer, my expanders were a preview of my reconstructed breasts, or so I thought. I liked what I saw, but was what I saw guaranteed? Hype and expectations about a movie can be misleading, and so can assumptions.

I called Dr. Holland's office and expressed my concern about size only to hear that my implants would feel more natural and softer to the touch. I was thankful for that because the expanders had made my chest feel as hard as rocks, and sleeping on my side left me bruised in the morning, but comfort wasn't as important as whether I would be a C cup. The nurse told me I should speak with Dr. Holland to discuss breast size. I ended the call and trusted I had filled enough to acquire the look I wanted.

My surgery was changed from late Friday morning to 6 AM, so I had to tweak the childcare arrangements. I'd arranged for our two older kids to stay with friends and for my youngest to stay with his sitter, Katrina Bonner. I hated to ask for favors, so I cringed when I asked the Kennedys, the Ludwigs, and Katrina if we could drop the kids off as early as 5 AM. They helped willingly. Playdates became sleepovers, and Katrina, our angel of a sitter, agreed to a 5 AM drop-off for Derek.

The alarm came too early for all three of us, but we were out the door by 4:45 to drop Derek off with Katrina and get on our way to Mount Carmel West. Ken drove, and I slept until he circled the car into the valet parking drop-off. Then we grabbed our belongings, headed into the hospital, and walked the same path we'd taken five months earlier. After registration, the déjà vu continued. Everything, from the room where I changed my clothes to the walk leading to the pre-op room, to the cubicle where I stayed before surgery, was identical, though today's surgery wouldn't be as intensive or prolonged.

Dr. Holland entered my cubicle and asked me to stand. To talk me through the procedure, he used a purple marker to mark directly under my expanders. These drawn lines would assist him in placing the implants. Next, he asked me whether he could make one incision about a half-inch longer to remove some scar tissue. I agreed, figuring *What's another half-inch to a three-inch scar as long as my bra or bikini top hides it?* It pleased me to know I'd be wheeled into the OR soon because I'd been the last patient last time, even though I was supposed to be the first. By 8:30 AM I was in surgery.

I awoke groggy and nauseated, and felt no immediate urge to see the results. The anesthesiologist had placed a patch behind my ear to decrease the nausea, so I was surprised by how sick I felt. Asked to rate my pain, I answered, "Five," assuming my decreased pain level was due to the loss of sensation in my breast area following the first surgery.

My curiosity piqued, I felt the contours of my chest. It felt flatter than I'd expected. I lifted the top of my surgical bra and I saw a gauze covering the length of my chest. It hid the peaks but not the valleys. Seeing the height of my new cleavage, I wanted to cry. Disappointment and anger filled me. I felt like the cartoon bull with steam coming out of his nose; I was the kid who'd told Santa exactly what she wanted only to receive something different. Dissatisfied, I wanted an immediate exchange, an impossible one. When the attending nurse gave me my implant cards, I saw the cc amount as 300. I questioned the amount, knowing my last fill had me up to 330cc. Little did I know that 30cc would have made no difference.

Ken had been right. Had I listened and completed more fills, I might be looking at bigger breasts, but the discomfort I'd experienced while running had made me stop. To give up running in trade for larger breasts wasn't an option. At the last fill, they'd looked big. The solidity of the expanders had given a false impression. My breasts, now softer, weren't as high as they'd been with the expanders.

Released by 1 PM, I was quiet on the way home. Ken knew I was livid and still reeling. He held my hand and focused on the road. Exasperated by my loss, angered by the betrayal of my trust, and disheartened by unfulfilled expectations, I called Dr. Holland's office. He was off, but I needed to voice my feelings. There would be no immediate answers, but I would question the results anyway. While the receptionist mentioned the possibility of complications due to thin skin, she said I would have to speak with Dr. Holland.

Once home, I faced the mirror in our master bathroom. I tightened the shirt fabric around my chest area and evaluated my figure. I wanted to sob. Vain? Aesthetics trumped vanity. I was altered and checkmated by adaptation. I had trusted Dr. Holland, my hired artist, to sculpt my breasts to be a close match, close enough to regain the curves that hid my small but visible baby belly.

Truthfully, Dr. Holland never had a chance. It was as though I'd shown the hair stylist a photo and expected the final result to convey the same glamour as the model pictured wearing the cut. The change was hard to visualize. Stylists fashion hair, but they have no control over facial shape, hair texture, body type, and age. What looks lovely on someone else might not look the same on you. Just as stylists suggest cuts suitable for clients, Dr. Holland had recommended a reconstruction that suited my body type, but I wanted the fantasy. As Henry David Thoreau wrote in his journal on July 2, 1857, "we find only the world we look for." The world I looked for had failed to materialize, but I wanted it anyway.

As if scrutinizing my figure in the mirror weren't torture enough, I went in for another defeating round, the fashion show. I tried on various clothes in my closet, posing in front of the full-length mirror on the back of our bedroom door. I hated clothes that used to outline my curves and exude sexiness. Instead, casual, career, and formal dresses hung on me. With nothing to fill out the top, I felt like Sandra Bullock in *The Proposal*, when Betty White refers to searching for Sandra's boobs as being like an Easter egg hunt. Unfortunately, I wasn't in a romantic comedy, and what I saw didn't make me laugh.

Stripping the clothes off my body didn't remove my psychological struggle. Discarded dresses and shirts became a mountain on my bed as the purge of my closet continued. Nothing I wore looked right anymore. I'd been handling this life-altering experience well, but a crack in my façade began to show again. If I assessed my worth by how my clothes fit, a new wardrobe wouldn't change how I felt. My body image, not my clothes, was the issue. My breasts dictated my mood and my relationship with my wardrobe. Until I came to terms with my new figure, I would find shopping for clothes worthless.

Turning to the Web, I perused images of well-known actresses chest sizes similar to mine. In their faces, I saw confidence. I needed to regain that sense of pride, but it would take time to embrace my new look. First, I needed to mourn. Until now, I had shrugged it off, poked fun, and disregarded the effects it would have on me.

At the follow-up appointment, Dr. Holland, who knew of my displeasure, offered to waive his fee for the additional surgery I needed within a year while my skin was still loose. He could not, however, speak to the other costs that would incur. He could increase my size, but beyond 100cc, I would need expanders. I saw the limitations when I looked at implants in my current size, 375cc and 400cc. As the cc's increased, the implants grew wider, not higher. Unlike the curvature of a normal breast, implants plateaued, rising from the chest wall to form a flat top. Conical implants, higher but not as wide at the base, looked less natural. An immediate decision wasn't necessary, but questions cycled.

Implants had limitations. I ignored those boundaries and focused on nonexistent possibilities. To seek perfection was a waste of time. Unlike the domed shape of normal breasts, silicone breasts were wide and flat. Increasing the size would expand my breasts outward, not up, and lead to bulging along the sides of my body. I was pleased with my breasts' symmetry and width, but the height failed to meet my expectations. Could I ever come to love what I had?

Dr. Holland wanted to set a date for nipple and areola reconstruction, and I chose one several months away. Initially, I'd visualized reconstruction from expanders to the tattooed areolas and skin-graft nipples. Now, this was less important to me. I still wanted bigger breasts without the additional surgery or inconveniences. I didn't want to be cut or have to deal with a week of drains again. What if I still wasn't pleased with the results? What if complications occurred? Would I regret my decision?

A few weeks later, at a birthday party for Ken's business colleague, I met another cancer survivor who suggested I have my areolas tattooed and my nipples skin grafted. At first, she hadn't wanted to have it done. She didn't want to be cut anymore but struggled to feel sexy. After those procedures, however, she felt sexier, and her sex drive returned. I felt sexy, nipples or no nipples. While I appreciated her sharing a personal decision, I wasn't sure this was the finishing touch for me. In God's eyes I was a work of art.

How I looked before my mastectomy was the standard I needed to let go of. Plastic surgery had failed to reconstruct that look. The perfection of my past was unattainable, yet hard to let go. Happy to have a chest, I resolved to accept my breasts. Rather than remain debilitated with anger for the world I'd lost, one with my natural breasts, I needed to celebrate the world I'd gained—my life.

Chapter Twenty-Five

A Different Kind of Hard

For I, the Lord your God, hold your right hand;
it is I who say to you, "Do not fear, I will help you."

—Isaiah 41:13 (NRSV)

One of my earliest recollections is of my dad reading to my two siblings and me before bedtime. We would fight over the prime position, his lap. Seated on my younger brother's queen bed, which served as the guest bedroom when we had visitors, Dad would have either side of him occupied while one of us sat on his lap. Eventually, we had to take turns. When he traveled for business, whether domestic or international, he read to us too, but overseas calls were expensive, and we were in different time zones. Hence his nightly reading came to us through a portable Emerson cassette recorder.

While we didn't have many books in our house, we had well-loved books, fought over, and filled with many lessons. Though *Harry the Dirty Dog*, *Gus Was A Friendly Ghost*, and *Curious George* topped my siblings' chart, my favorite by far was Watty Piper's *The Little Engine That Could*. The cover's texture and the vibrant yet subtle pastel watercolor illustrations drew me into the book. Dad's voice danced rhythmically over the words while he inserted his chugga-chugga-chugga-choo-choo sounds as each train made its way up and over the mountain. Most of all, I loved how my father's voice portrayed the little blue engine for the strong character she was.

Like the little blue engine, I never wanted to be conquered, yet challenges fueled my competitive spirit. When others told me something wasn't possible, I found the possible. I disregarded their words and I listened to mine. I took the chance, and I made it happen. That's not to say I won every situation, but I entered each with that intention and drive.

My competitive spirit and undeterred mindset led me to the moment of registration for the Columbus Marathon. As I typed in my personal information, I thought, *Naysayers be damned!* My chemotherapy and reconstructive surgery were complete. I entered my credit card information, clicked the button, and smiled, knowing my entry was official. There was no turning back!

When I printed out my receipt, I wanted to frame it. I wanted to tell everyone I knew that I would run this marathon. With sixty-five days left to train, I was itching to run again, but a doctor-ordered two-week hiatus halted me. Unfortunately, walking didn't cut it, but disregarding the doctor's orders would only put me in a pay-me-now-or-pay-me-later situation. I'd worked too hard to let impatience rob me of my golden moment.

When Dr. Holland cleared me to run, I had to start slow. He'd told me to increase my mileage and pace based on how I felt, so I began gingerly on a gorgeous Monday morning. Unsure how my chest might feel, I felt like an athlete trying out a new pair of shoes. The expanders had felt awkward, and I determined my last fill when it hurt me to run. Though fake, my chest felt normal when I ran, but I didn't want to overdo it. I felt no repercussions from the previous day, so I ran five miles. As the week progressed, I added a mile each day. It was exhilarating, and the two-week break didn't affect my speed. By Saturday, I ran twelve miles with Derek in the baby jogger. To celebrate, I did my *Rocky*. While I wasn't atop the steps in front of the Philadelphia Museum of Art, I had crested Yaples Orchard Drive, a daunting, steep half-mile incline. Holding my hands over my head, I punched the air while I hopped from one foot to the other. Earned, it was a beautiful moment. It didn't matter that I looked crazy to the passing drivers.

Derek peeked around the running stroller, looked at me, and shouted, "No stop! Go fast, Mommy!"

Granting his wishes, I put my hands on the handle and sprinted home. Anxiety diminished, I thought, *Boston, here I come!*

I was not only back running but was also back in my classroom. Thankfully, I wasn't riffed or dismissed. Instead, I prepared for the new school year. I organized my materials and began to plan for a new grade level. With the desks already in order, since I couldn't lift anything heavy for another two weeks, I covered my bulletin boards and decorated my room. Staff members who peeked into my classroom expressed their relief and happiness to see me.

Our school's opening convocation for staff occurs yearly in the high-school auditorium. January, the last time I'd sat in that auditorium, I hid behind a lying smile. Clueless as to what stage I was, whether radiation or chemotherapy would be necessary, or if I'd have to leave my job, I maneuvered carefully through the day. My mental status had been a minefield, and my conversations a blur. Nearly nine months had passed, but I remembered the raw emotion. While a high school girl's singing *Over the Rainbow* made me think of dreams, my cancer made me feel defeated.

I parked in the side lot and walked to the school's front entrance. While I had finished my treatments, I still showed signs that I'd had cancer. My hair was between short stubble and a pixie cut. I wore a navy-blue newsboy hat instead of my Nike Dri-Fit Featherlight cap. As I walked through the parking lot, the school entrance, and the auditorium doors, I was approached by Allen Elementary and Chillicothe Middle School colleagues. The last time they'd seen me was last January. They welcomed me back warmly, and commented on how wonderful I looked.

After the convocation, I had to return to my school for a luncheon followed by a staff meeting. On the way to my car, I heard someone call my name. I turned around and saw Pam, a colleague I'd known since my first teaching assignment in Chillicothe as a tutor of English as a Second Language for two Japanese students, a brother and sister. We met at Allen Elementary, where Pam worked as a reading specialist. Until she kindly offered me a spot in her room, I'd worked in the hallway with the brother, a third grader. Pam offered me advice and support throughout the year as I sought a full-time teaching position.

There on the sidewalk, we exchanged pleasantries, and Pam told me how much she had thought about me and how great it was to see me back. She'd now sought me for another reason, however: Her husband, Larry, had just been diagnosed with kidney cancer. As Pam told me how they'd found out and how the doctor informed Larry, it was plain to see how heavily this weighed on her. She asked about my experience with chemotherapy. I told her that a positive attitude, faith in God, and exercise had made the difference. I suffered few side effects, and had experienced very little fatigue.

Larry's diagnosis was daunting. I could see the concern on her face and hear the fear in her voice. Cancer isn't an easy word to hear. It makes the world stop spinning, and the hourglass sands halt. The images and presumptive path are less than uplifting. Like the grim reaper with his scythe, a skeletal figure cloaked in black doom, cancer smothers the future. Upon arrival, it brings darkness that makes it hard to see the light. Pam's story brought me back to mine. I knew she was still processing, but I hoped our talk brought her the light and positivity she needed to keep faith and hope alive.

Being the spouse of a cancer patient is most difficult. As a patient, you must overcome an illness and are subject to many physical and mental side effects that wreak havoc on you. The spouse, however, is thrown into the hamster wheel and tries to maintain the roles he or she has always played—husband or wife, mother or father, stay-at-home caregiver, or working provider—while caring for a sick loved one. At times, the spouse can be more nervous for the patient than the patient is for herself. A spouse puts his needs aside to monitor and care for a loved one. As a result, the spouse, though in need of the same concern and attention the patient receives, can be overlooked.

As a patient, all the attention is on you. Doctors monitor your health. In my case, I had three plus nurse practitioners. In addition, I had the cell number of my medical oncologist, which he gave out to all his Adena cancer patients. Besides doctors, I had other support services. Ellen, a nurse navigator, was assigned to me the day I found out my diagnosis, and Sue, my care manager from CoreSource, my health-care provider. Ellen helped me with the medical appointments, and Sue called me every week before and after the surgery to check my mental state. During appointments and calls, each ensured I knew she was there for me. If I had any questions or concerns, I would call them. Finally, I had the support of family and friends who lovingly showered me with cards, letters, emails, care packages, and phone calls.

During my cancer ordeal, Ken kept to himself, his thoughts in a vault, just like mine. He didn't tell people around him. Sometimes, the stress showed in his arguments with the kids. He wanted to be a rock for me. Finally, after I'd completed all the recommended treatments, he admitted that he was afraid for me, and that the day of my double mastectomy was the longest day of his life.

Before we parted, I told Pam I would pray for her and her husband. In addition, I told her to reach out if she needed anything, such as advice, meals, or being a good listener. Leaving, I made a mental note to email her in a week or two. Like me, Pam was strong. She'd approached me today, but I knew she wouldn't reach out for help even though I offered. Strong people don't like to feel they're imposing on anyone. It's best to be insistent and assertive. Make a plan. Schedule the dinner drop. Call. Ask, "How are you doing?" Don't leave an open invitation—it will remain unanswered.

My first week back was terrific. I was back to a routine, doing the job I loved. While I'd missed finishing the year with my fifth graders, I had the chance to teach them again as sixth graders. As for my hair, they didn't care if I chose to go with or without a hat. My stubble didn't faze them. They were just glad to have me back.

Chapter Twenty-Six

The Proving Ground

The only person you are destined to become is the person you decide to be.

—Ralph Waldo Emerson

I'd been involved in sports all my life, and sports taught me many lessons. First, you need passion to persevere and succeed. Second, defeat is humbling, trial-and-error produces results, grit can beat the powerhouse, and winning exhilarates. Last, injuries will happen, and fear can cripple. While I never reached the professional level in any sport, the lessons and values of sports don't distinguish between recreational, amateur, and elite athletes.

Beyond the lessons and values, sports are inspirational. If you had asked me what sports movie I found most uplifting when I was young, it would have been *Chariots of Fire*. Vangelis's theme song made me feel like anything was possible. When I heard it, I imagined myself performing flawless gymnastic routines like Nadia Comaneci on the bar, beam, vault, and, my favorite, floor. I became a runner through gymnastics, but it would be easy to credit the movie.

With time, however, comes change. Now, *Rudy* is the sports movie I find most inspirational. While there have been many inspirational sports films such as *Rocky*, *Hoosiers*, *A League of Their Own*, and *Field of Dreams*, *Rudy* brings tears to my eyes no matter how many times I watch it. I love Daniel "Rudy" Ruetteger's leap of faith as he leaves behind the security of his family and job to pursue his dream of playing football at Notre Dame. Undeterred by his lack of top grades, money, talent, or physical stature, as well as the lack of family support, Rudy's grit and the people who supported him—Pete, Fortune, D-Bob, and Father Cavanaugh—made his dream attainable. Every step of the way, obstacles could have prevented Rudy's achievements, but like the little blue train, he had the courage. Little did I know that a Rudy encounter was about to occur.

I faced hesitancy from naysayers even after I signed up for the Columbus Marathon. Then, during a thirteen-mile run with the group I'd joined after the Fire Run, I overheard some members talking about a twenty-mile run in Columbus in September. This run would calm the fears and concerns of my naysayers, so I signed up for the race.

The morning of the run was overcast and the humidity was low. My cheerleaders, Ken, Aleya, and Derek, came with me. We parked, and I saw Jen and Jerry, members of the running group. I left the car to get my bib number, shirt, and other registration goodies. Then I went to talk to Jen, Jerry, and the other group members who were arriving. I stretched and ran warm-up laps around the parking lot with them.

Meanwhile, near the registration tables, Ken spotted Sean Astin, who'd portrayed Rudy. We had just watched the movie a few nights before the race. Here for the Wizard World Ohio Comic Con in Columbus, Sean had decided to race. Instead of the twenty-miler, he'd chosen to run the ten-miler so as to return in time for his Comic-Con commitments. Ken was enamored by famous people, and asked Sean for a picture of him holding Derek. Sean took hold of Derek while Ken prepared his phone for the shot. Then, prompted by Derek's shy finger-in-the-mouth pose, Sean did the same. Later, Ken printed the photo and hung it on the refrigerator door.

Near the start time, I made my way to the line. Due to the smaller group of runners, there were no corrals. I stood a few rows back from the front to avoid mixing in with the faster male and female runners like Jen and Jerry. With the gun start, I kept with the middle pack. For the twenty-miler, I would run a ten-mile gravel-trail loop twice. Surrounded by the spectacular colors of fall foliage, and hearing the crunch of the gravel as my feet hit the ground, made for ideal course conditions. The scenery, quiet and gorgeous, was mesmerizing.

While I ran the first ten-mile loop, I saw no hydration stations. I thought this odd. Most races of this distance had them. I'd seen large quantities of water bottles by the registration table, and assumed volunteers would provide water along the course. Fortunately, I had worn my hydration belt with two six-ounce bottles of Gatorade.

As I neared the end of that first loop, I saw Jen start her second. We cheered for each other. When I reached the corner that completed the first ten-mile loop, I saw Ken, Aleya, and Derek cheering for me. I would see them again when I finished. Beginning the second loop, I saw Sean Astin finish. I wasn't big on celebrities, but took joy in the knowledge that I'd beaten "Rudy."

I felt great, and kept a comfortable pace. While this race served nicely as a twenty-mile training run for members of my running group, it was the proving ground to show I was ready for a marathon. When I used to run independently, I found the longer runs, anything beyond ten, grueling and tedious. Races and group runs became the perfect scenarios for a longer training run.

By mile 17, I was starting to experience a headache and side stitches. My Gatorade gone, I had no hydration or fuel such as gels or food. I'd never trained with gels because I always worried my stomach wouldn't handle them well, so I had only trained with Gatorade. Unfortunately, my symptoms suggested dehydration and depleted glycogen levels.

Three miles from the finish line, I steadily declined, feeling the dreaded wall. I fought, however, because I was the little engine that could, and there was no way I would quit. This race was proof to me as much as to my naysayers, and quitting would only make a case for them. I had come too far to let that happen. How would I finish, though, without Gatorade or food?

Fortunately, I had an angel on the trail. He noticed my struggles and, as he reached me, asked how I was. I told him of my ailments, and he offered me one of his gel packets. I took it and thanked him. As he ran ahead, I thought about how he'd saved me from an ugly ending. Once the gel took effect, my headache and stomach cramps subsided.

As my symptoms vanished, I thought about God's presence. He made me feel like I was constantly on his radar. He looked after me. Since my diagnosis, He had sent many messages. First, there was the candle; then there was GRACE, and finally, the cardinals in the trees around my house. This made me wonder if He had sent the man with the gel. And what about Sean Astin? Was Rudy a coincidence too? It seemed appropriate that the inspirational underdog was there, even though Sean Astin wasn't the actual Rudy. He reminded me that you're not out even when you're down. All that mattered was my ability, heart, soul, and belief in myself. They always were and always would be my sources of inspiration.

I saw the finish line and heard my cheerleaders loud and clear. Sprinting with everything I had left, I imagined Eric Liddell from *Chariots of Fire* racing the 400-meter run at the

1924 Olympics. In the scene, he reflects upon how the power to complete the race comes from within oneself. From within my mind, I repeated, "I thought I could, I thought I could," all the way to the glorious arch of the finish.

Chapter Twenty-Seven

Hero

A hero is a man who does what he can.

—Romain Rolland

As a kid, I loved espionage shows like *Charlie's Angels*, *The A-Team*, *The Bionic Woman*, *MacGyver*, *Scarecrow and Mrs. King*, and *Airwolf*. My favorite, though short-lived, was *Cover Up*. As I watched the opening and listened to the lyrics of the theme song, *Holding Out for a Hero*, I saw a hero, the strong, handsome Jon-Erik Hexum, wade through the water like Rambo. When I was growing up, heroes depicted in fairy tales and other stories were muscular and attractive, so if you had asked me, as a youngster, what a hero was, I would've responded, "Someone who saves you from a life-threatening situation."

Then came cancer. Suddenly, the word "hero" was being used to describe me. Hero? Me? No. How could I be a hero? I was a cancer patient, not someone saving someone else's life. "Hero" was too strong a term for me. It's a term reserved for men and women who made a difference at the risk of their own lives. Martin Luther King Jr., an American Baptist minister and leader of the Civil Rights Movement, was a hero. Irena Sendler, a Polish social worker and nurse who risked her life to smuggle thousands of Jewish children out of the Warsaw ghetto and into hiding, was a hero. Iqbal Masih, a Pakistani boy who, forced into bond labor at four, fought child labor and helped free thousands of enslaved children before his death at twelve, was a hero. Malala Yousafzai, an education activist from Pakistan whom the Taliban tried to kill, is a hero. Lewis Hines, an American sociologist and photographer whose documented images of child labor in the early 1900s helped reform child labor laws, was a hero. The 9/11 first responders, FDNY firefighters and paramedics, Port Authority, New York, and New Jersey police were heroes. The brave men and women of the armed services who protect us today and serve to protect us and others worldwide are heroes. These are just a few examples of men, women, and children worldwide who exemplify the definition of "hero."

While some called me a hero, others called me a medical marvel, but I don't believe I was one. I want to think I was the little pig in the brick house. While I let the big bad wolf of TC (Taxotere and Cytoxan) in, my body and all its systems gave the drugs clear instructions about how we handled things in our house: "You do your job and we'll do ours. Don't think of interfering with what we need to do and this arrangement will work out just fine."

In addition to being a hero and a medical marvel, they called me inspirational. While I never thought having cancer could inspire others, I was glad a positive could come from a negative. If I struggled to inspire anyone, I hoped it was my daughter. God willing, I hoped Aleya would never experience breast cancer; if, however, she did, I hoped my example would lead her to tackle this disease as I had. In addition, I wished my children would learn from my example what to do in a harsh and uncomfortable situation. If anything, this was my lesson to them.

As for my inspiration, Mary Bryant, I never met her, but when I read that she'd run the New York City Marathon four months after her mastectomy and six days after her fifth round of chemotherapy, she put my dream back on the table. Though further out from my mastectomy and chemo treatments, I would run my third marathon, my hill, the hill other trains told the little blue train, me, was impossible. Today I would climb and descend to the finish line.

With the sun still asleep, Ken dropped me off near the starting corrals and went to look for a parking spot closer to the finish. Leaving the warmth of the car, I felt the chilly 38-degree autumn morning. By race time, 38 degrees would creep into the low 40s, a perfect temperature to run a race.

Unlike my son, Trent, who'd run in poor conditions the day before, I had perfect weather. I couldn't have asked for better conditions: No rain, a clear sky, and minimal wind. Unfortunately, Trent wasn't so lucky. Running with Division 1 schools at the Ohio Junior High State Cross Country Championships, he'd run in extremely cold and rainy conditions in his team's tank top and shorts. Considering the elements, I marveled at how he'd run two miles in 12:06, placing 47th out of 184 runners.

I followed the crowd of runners an hour and a half before the start, and sought a warm spot and the porta-potty with the shortest line. Wait too long to visit a porta-potty and you'd wait in an extremely long line. Then you'd worry about whether you could make it inside the corral before the start, or contemplate using a porta-potty along the course. The second was not an option. Focused on time, I wanted to run nonstop. Fortunately, I found a row of porta-potties farther from the starting corrals where minimal runners waited to use them.

I tried to calm myself, but the butterflies fluttered in my stomach, where they would remain until mile 1 or 2. With this nervousness came the constant sensation that I had to pee. I used a porta-potty more than once before the start and was in no rush to leave. For some reason, out of any distance race, I experienced nervous energy only for the marathon.

With half an hour to go, I left my warm spot and headed toward the corral. I did a few more running stretches outside the corral area and checked my laces. An eighteen-week training plan had led to this moment. Minus the two-week hiatus in August and a slow start back, I'd followed the plan. While the twenty-miler in September had boosted my confidence, I felt a tinge of doubt seep through: Did I do enough to produce a personal best?

Today, I was one of 7,000 marathon runners. According to a Columbus Expo speaker who spoke Friday afternoon, I was a minority. Statistically, I was one half of one percent of the U.S. population that has run a marathon. It made me wonder how much lower the percentage would have dropped among cancer survivors. In terms of the world population, I was in the one-hundredth percentile. Running a marathon was a one-and-done check-off the bucket list for some runners. Training and competing were passions for other runners who loved the sport. Then there were runners like me, who planned to run the race once but changed their minds after the finish. Boston changed my mind. There would be no stopping until Boston.

I made my way into corral C and spotted a pacer holding the 3:45 placard. As a group began to form, I decided to stay close, unsure whether I would run with them. I put in my earphones, checked my Garmin, and retied and double knotted my laces. I was ready. While various speakers spoke, I continued to stretch and felt nervous. As the national anthem was sung, more runners made their way into the corrals.

Then, AC/DC's *Thunderstruck* blasted over the speakers. A few runners jumped up and down. Others chanted, "Thunder ah ah ah ah ah ah ah! Thunder ah ah ah ah ah ah ah!"

In the air, I saw sweatshirts and robes used to keep runners warm in the cold pre-race hour thrown over the barricades. Some runners kept on their Mylar blankets and plastic bags for warmth. I decided to keep the old fleece jacket Ken had given me a bit longer. Later, volunteers would collect the discarded clothes for Goodwill.

Thunderstruck ended and a cannon boomed. A display of pyrotechnics shot off from the aluminum truss starting line, and Springsteen's *Born to Run* pierced the air while runners in every tightly packed corral started to move. Going from a walk to a slow jog, I hit a running gait as I passed the starting line. Shoulder to shoulder with other runners, I was mindful of my pace. The excitement and the crowd's energy made it easy to go too fast and start to weave around slower runners, which wasted energy and added extra distance in the end.

As I ran down East Broad Street, I knew I would do a small out and back until mile 8. Spectators lined both sides of the road. Between miles 2 and 3, I started to have more distance between other runners and me, and I could see the wheelchair-division leaders on the other side of the street, at mile 7. Turning left off Broad, I passed the governor's mansion before mile 4 led into Bexley, an old tree-lined suburb of Columbus. I made a right turn onto East Main, passed Capital University, and returned down East Broad.

As I passed the hydration stations, I chose Gatorade over water. The volunteers extended their arms as we ran past so we could grab a cup. I pinched the top of the cup in the middle and drank. This system worked better when trying to run and drink simultaneously. Then I threw the cup to the side, out of the way of the runners behind me.

I left German Village and entered mile 11, the Angel Mile. As sobering as it was uplifting, the Angel Mile was a dedication mile to the Angels who were no longer here. Along South High Street in the Brewery District, the Angel families came together to support one another, honor their Angels, and cheer for the runners. Parents and grandparents held signs with pictures of their dear loved ones. The ones with the adorable baby pictures, like Zackery, tugged at my heart. I tried not to cry. I couldn't imagine losing a child, let alone one who hadn't even reached their first birthday.

Then I noticed a sign with foam butterflies and the message REMEMBER WHY U RUN. I thought about cancer and how grateful I was for my life. I knew that some of these Angels, whose signs had various colored ribbons, had been afflicted by the disease. If any marathon was worth running, it was this one. At no point could you feel sorry for yourself or fall into a defeated mindset, because kids who were dealing with illnesses were there along the way to remind you what strength, courage, and resilience looked like.

I reached mile 13 and watched a few of the 11,000 half marathoners split from the full marathoners to run a tenth of a mile to the finish line. I passed the halfway mark and thought about how I viewed my chemotherapy like the last half of a marathon. In letters to family and friends, I termed the therapy weeks and the weeks between them in terms of miles. I started at mile 14. Four rounds of chemotherapy with twenty-one days between gave me eighty-four days or twelve weeks. Mile 23, following my fourth treatment and the Fire Run, was the last group letter I sent.

At mile 15, I saw my cheering section, Ken and the kids. Ken took pictures and asked how I felt. I gave him a thumbs-up. While some runners stopped to kiss, hug, or talk to their spouses and children, I kept running to keep my pace time on target. I looked at my Garmin and saw that my mile pace had been a consistent 8:35, and I still felt strong.

I'd run this race twice before, so I knew I was coming up to the stretch I liked least, the Ohio State Stadium loop. It wasn't because I was a Penn State graduate. Miles 16 through 19 dragged. There was very little crowd support outside the hydration stations, the patient champion tent areas, and the bridge where runners cheered on runners as they passed them on the opposite side. During these miles, negative thoughts try to penetrate the mind.

Nearing mile 17, I felt the wind come at me as I ran over the bridge toward the stadium. In the previous marathons, I'd run around the stadium, but this year I had to run down a 45-degree concrete ramp. Then, after passing the goal post, I had to run back up another 45-degree concrete ramp. Some were excited to enter the stadium, nicknamed the 'Shoe (short for Horseshoe), but I was irritated by the sloped entrance and exit. It slowed me down and made me worry about the impact on my knees. Lastly, the sharp incline made me feel tired.

I knew that my pace had slowed, so I kept saying positive words to keep away the negative feelings associated with the dreaded wall. I wanted a personal best, which meant I had to maintain an 8:35 pace time, but I had yet to be able to do this since mile 15. Under a nine-minute mile pace, I wanted to keep it that way. I kept repeating, "I am the little blue engine! Let's go!" and "I had cancer! It did not beat me! I can do this!"

Mile 20 meant more crowds as runners neared the final 10K that took them through Upper Arlington, Grand View Heights, and the Victorian Village. Seeing the mile 20 marker gave me a spark of exhilaration. Almost done—I could do this! The spark was extinguished, however, by a wave of reality when I saw the 3:45 and, eventually, the four-hour pace group, pass me in the stretch of miles 21–22. Boston wasn't going to happen, but making the finish line was.

As my legs began to feel heavier, I pushed my pace as much as possible. I knew my pace times had fallen into the 11-minute miles. I refused to look at my Garmin. Instead, I repeatedly told myself, "You can do this, you're strong, and you'll finish!" Sometimes I felt my walking pace would be faster than my jog, but I refused to walk. It was disheartening to see other runners walk and then pass me as they started to run again. Tired, I tried not to think about it. My main goal was to finish and have a finisher's medal placed around my neck.

As I approached the Arena District, I noticed the growing crowds. Their cheers and the glorious sounds of the cowbells energized me. Then, I saw the mile 25 sign. Tears of pride streaked my cheeks. The grand finish was a little over a mile, slightly more than four laps of a track from my goal of completion.

The roars of the crowd grew louder as I made the final turn. Then, I saw the word FINISH in big, black letters. A word never looked so exciting. Under it was the line that represented my journey, the line some had said wasn't possible to cross this year. It would be my touchdown, spike the ball, and in-your-face moment when I crossed it. All I had to do was run it home.

I dug deep and ran with everything I had left. The shouts and the cowbells led me closer. I swung my arms next to me, trying to create more power as I saw the seconds of the timer ticking. Then I kicked it in, and felt a surge of energy as I sprinted on tired legs.

I crossed the rubber timing mat and stopped my Garmin. I didn't achieve the Hollywood ending, didn't cross the finish line in 3 hours and 45 minutes, my Boston qualifying time, but my family stood cheering, waving, and taking pictures of me from behind the barricades. They were proud. Accepting my finisher's medal, I felt slightly defeated. I'd accomplished a momentous feat, though not a personal best, but it was 26.2 miles, the 26.2 miles others had told me not to run. In 4 hours and 9 minutes, I had completed my possible and others' impossible. Cancer did not win; I did. My third marathon finisher's medal was the title belt I'd earned and would cherish forever.

On the ride home, I ate a little from the bag of food I'd been given in the Athlete's Village. Then I fell asleep. Once home, I felt like the rusty Tin Man as I exited the car; I had to use my arms to move my legs out the door. Then I stood up and did a slow Frankenstein walk to the house. Once inside, I made my way to the foyer. Stairs, never a runner's friend, came between a much-deserved shower and me.

After a shower, I opened my laptop to write an email to friends and family, but before I could compose it, I saw a message in my inbox from Emilia. Based on her email the day before, I knew she planned to follow me through an app that allowed her to track my progress. Her message had said, "I'll be following you and cheering you on from afar! I hope your experience is even better than you could imagine. You're amazing!"

I opened her email and read:

Hi Gwyn,
You are my hero! How do you make time for all you do especially training for this marathon? Knowing you, I'm sure there's at least one thing about the marathon that you wish you'd done differently or had gone better, but you're still one of the most amazing women I know. I am truly blessed to call you my friend!

Get some rest and enjoy your day!
Emilia

I took a two-week break so my body could recuperate from the marathon. Afterward, I joined the running group for an early Tuesday morning run. They wanted to hear about my marathon experience. When I mentioned my disappointment over not attaining a Boston qualifying time, Pam, who ran alongside me, shot me a look that could've stopped any of us mid-stride.

Then she said, "Are you (expletive) kidding me? You had (expletive) cancer!"

The group went silent.

"You're right," I responded.

That ended my dwelling on a time I couldn't change. Sometimes you find perspective in places you least expect.

Chapter Twenty-Eight

From Victim to Victor

Conquer yourself rather than the world.

—Rene Descartes

In fifth grade, a letter addressed to me changed my friendship circle. It spoke of my personality. Daggers such as *childish*, *immature*, and *silly* described why the letter's author could no longer be my friend. It made me cry. I felt alone and frightened, and pondered whether I'd be ostracized.

The letter ended up under my bed in my Grandma Vi's vintage two-tiered Mele jewelry box. Especially drawn to the lock and key, I asked to have it when Grandma wanted to discard it. I took it home, and put it under my bed to store my treasures. I kept my babysitting money on the top shelf, and on the bottom, special items such as my gymnastic ribbons and medals. Only that day it came to hold something negative, a letter saying I wasn't worthy of someone's friendship.

Popularity was the reason. Association with me hurt my friend's chances. The friend who'd written the letter left with another friend who felt it was in her best interest to go too, so our friendship coterie split into one group of two and one of six.

I reread the letter one time too many. Eventually, after weeks of torture, I tore it up like I should've done the first day, and threw it away for the trash it was. No one had the right to define me. God molded me in His image. I would not be tarnished!

I should have shown the letter to an adult, but I did not. Growing up, I often heard the phrase "Sticks and stones may break my bones, but names will never hurt me." I wondered who had come up with this phrase, because I wanted to refute it. Words have an impact. Disease isn't the only thing that seeks to break you. Sometimes words hurt worse than a bruise or a break. As for the healing period, unkind comments can leave lasting damage.

Rosemary, one of the five who remained, approached me in the recess yard and said, "You're worth more to me than popularity. What's popularity anyway? It's an opinion, that's all."

While it was hard to lose what I thought were true friends, the experience showed me who my real friends were. Rosemary's words healed the dagger's wounds and taught me that friendship was worth more than social status.

Just like that letter, hearing the doctor say, "I am concerned. I am very concerned," shocked me and hurt me to my core. My cancer diagnosis made me feel like a victim, the victim I loathed being. Victims are controlled. To be a victim means you've lost. I lost the opportunity to run a spring marathon, finish my school year, and hold my toddler for a month. In addition, I lost my breasts, a part of my sensuality, and my sexual starters. Cancer took up full-time residence in my brain for the first few weeks. By letting cancer access my psyche, I let it pummel my self-esteem, dampen my outlook, and make me hide the truth.

Being a victim, however, is not too far from being a victor. It's just the other side of the coin. Both words derive from the Latin root *-vict-*, meaning *conquer*. The conquered versus the conqueror. With the statement "Apparently, breast cancer didn't know whose body it decided to attack, because I am a formidable opponent," I flipped control and became the conqueror.

Though my attitude hit a few speed bumps along the way, it chose to be victorious.

Yes, the disease victimized my body. It invaded my left breast without permission causing me to lose both. It came. It took. It left. It scarred my physical appearance, but I stayed who I was. My body didn't define me. My soul did. Even when a body dies due to the disease, cancer never wins. Why? Cancer can't kill your soul unless you let it.

Life is a controlled journey in a society that trains one to believe that the future is moldable. Even after situations arose that I held no control over, people told me I'd overseen the pieces and my path. When I was a high school junior, my English teacher asked me to write a composition sharing where I saw myself in ten years. Asked why I hadn't included marriage or kids, I replied that I wasn't in charge of another person's life and therefore couldn't plan another's future. In a sense, the project, while forward-thinking, was an oxymoron. A person can plan for the future, but it's not his or hers to control. As a teenager, I didn't see myself attending a state university, running a marathon, or being a breast cancer survivor. As one of a graduating class of 103 students, I found the prospect of a state university overwhelming. Had my dad not insisted I apply to a state school, I wouldn't have had the opportunity to attend Penn State. Had I not felt the need for competition after Aleya's birth, I wouldn't have started to run road races that led to a bigger goal, the full marathon. As for breast cancer, no one in my family had had it, so why would I think it could have been in my future?

The lesson? Life wasn't a board game. Unlike "The Game of Life" created by Milton Bradley, you couldn't start from the beginning, have a redo, forget your earlier life, or cheat. It wasn't MASH, the paper fortune-telling game commonly played when I was a child, in which a number would determine what car you would drive, the size of your future home, whom you would marry, and how many kids you'd have. My whole life, I had seen the future as something you planned, even though there had been times when I wasn't in control.

For as long as I can remember, I've been a big believer in fate, much to my husband's chagrin. Situations have arisen where my saying that things happen for a reason makes Ken cringe. Perhaps believing there's a purpose is why I've been happy even in times of struggle. Journeys and difficult decisions are sometimes placed in one's path for a reason. When I look back at certain times in my life, I see the significance of these events. If I hadn't gone to the YMCA while Mom was doing aerobics, I wouldn't have witnessed gymnastics and fallen in love with the sport. If I hadn't asked my parents to register me for gymnastics classes, I wouldn't have experienced the joy of running. Had I not yearned for the thrill of competition and earning awards, I might have never started road races later in life. If I hadn't started to run road races, I wouldn't have thought about running a marathon. Had I not trained and run a marathon, I might not have had the fortitude to face cancer.

As the Roman emperor and Stoic philosopher Marcus Aurelius wrote, "Adapt thyself to the things with which thy lot has been cast; and the men among whom thou hast received thy portion, love them, but do it truly [sincerely]." His words reflect one of the Stoic concepts, *Amor Fati*, which translates as "love of fate" and describes an attitude that accepts and embraces all life's experiences as good, including suffering and loss. The word "love" struck me because love can overcome every other force.

As a Catholic, I grew up learning to love my enemy as myself. Cancer was an enemy. While I didn't love cancer, I loved what it brought to the fore in me. Cancer surfaced my strength, highlighted my resilience, and showcased a determined woman unwearied by obstacles; a woman who chose to laugh and smile after a day or two of tears and anger. First Corinthians

13:7(NRSV) states that love "bears all things, believes all things, hopes all things, endures all things." It's true. My love for God and trust in Him enabled me to endure cancer without giving up hope.

God presented me with a hurdle to start 2013. While my struggle lasted more than the biblical forty days, it lasted less than forty years. In the beginning, I wanted to keep my diagnosis hidden. Caught off guard, I was silent. I didn't know how to proceed with the scant information I had. Facing a hurdle is not about its height but the leap of faith needed to clear it. To fear is to waste time. If one fears, then it becomes one's focus. 2013 helped me become more focused on important matters rather than monotonous ones.

Now, as the countdown to the New Year, 2014, began, I was surrounded by my family in a car in a parking lot that overlooked Gatlinburg, Tennessee. As I gazed at the iconic Gatlinburg Space Needle, I had much to be thankful for, and was ready to put more emphasis on the rocks than on the pebbles. Perfection was no longer on my radar. It would always be unattainable. Being human, I know and perform imperfectly, so why strive for what I'm not and never will be?

Ready to leave 2013 behind, I watched the ball slowly drop from atop the Space Needle. As Mary Tyler Moore had in her show's title sequence, I felt like tossing my hat. I was going to make it. Indeed, I had. I will stay focused on my journey, not the end or the strife encountered. I will rejoice in being an imperfect being made in the image of God until I cross the finish line of my mission in God's eyes and return to my Heavenly home. For now, however, as I watched the ball stop and the fireworks explode, I wanted to hear *We Are the Champions* by Queen rather than the traditional New Year's song *Auld Lang Syne*. I was a champion! Ringing in 2014 in Gatlinburg, Tennessee, with kisses, hugs, and a smile, I looked forward to remaining victorious.

Permissions

Dyer, Wayne W. *The Power of Intention: Learning to Co-Create Your World Your Way.* Carlsbad, CA: Hay House LLC, 2004. Quoted courtesy of Hay House.

[Scripture quotations are from] New Revised Standard Version Bible, copyright © 1989 National Council of the Churches of Christ in the United States of America. Used by permission. All rights reserved worldwide.

Campbell, Joseph. *Reflections on the Art of Living: A Joseph Campbell Companion.*
New York: Harper Perennial, 1991, p. 20. For more information about Joseph Campbell, visit jcf.org. Quoted courtesy of the Joseph Campbell Foundation.

About the Author

A thirteen-year breast cancer survivor, Gwyn grew to love running at a young age. She trains for and races in various distances annually, including her favorite, the half marathon. Last fall, she met her Boston qualifying time and ran her first international Abbott World Marathon Major this spring. She is training for her twenty-first marathon. *Run, Mommy, Run* is her first book.

Instagram: runspirellc